Major League Praise for Baseball Instructi[c]

"This is one of the very best instructional books on not only the game but teaching the game that has come across our editorial desk and offers something for everyone at all levels of the game."

— BASEBALL THE MAGAZINE

"What I find refreshing about your book is your candid discussions on your struggles vs. successes and your willingness/ability to learn more from your losses than your wins, so to speak. I suppose this has a lot to do with your drive as an instructor over the years — unlike better–known MLB vets who perhaps never had to challenge themselves and whose books are more "pat answers" than constructive help. Those personal insights make you much more helpful."

— RICHARD TODD, WEB BALL (ONLINE STORE)

"He (Jack) smack's one out of the park and into the parking lot with this outstanding book on hitting, coaching and parenting."

"There is not a better teaching guide available on hitting a baseball for players at all levels and being a successful coach and teacher on and off the field."

— RICHARD CORENO, AMAZON REVIEWER

"Whether you play tee ball or master's league softball, whether you're a coach or a parent, if the goal is hitting a ball with a bat there's a gold mine of information in "The Making of a Hitter,' a new book by former major leaguer Jack Perconte."

— DAVE OBERHELMAN, DAILY HERALD – CHICAGO SUBURBAN NEWSPAPER

"I just wish I had it (The Making of a Hitter) for all those years when my daughter Sarah and son Matt were young, and I tried to teach them and their teammates a little about hitting."

— DICK GOSS, CHICAGO SUBURBAN NEWS EDITOR – JOLIET HERALD NEWS

"Here is what Perconte does best. Most of all, he breaks the swing down into words that can be understood."

"Speaking from experience, this book is a grand slam."

— KEVIN KERNAN, NEW YORK POST

"In the pressure — packed world of competitive youth sports, it is a pleasure to read the words of a man who places kids first."

— BRUCE WASSER, AMAZON REVIEWER

The Making of a Hitter

A Proven and Practical Step-by-Step Baseball Guide

Former Major Leaguer
Jack Perconte

Published by Second Base Publishing, P.O. Box 3012 Lisle, IL 60532

Publisher's Cataloging-in-Publication
(Provided by Quality Books, Inc.)

Perconte, Jack.
    The making of a hitter : a proven and practical
step-by-step baseball guide / Jack Perconte ; foreword
by Mike Scioscia.
      p. cm.
      LCCN 2008905145
      ISBN-13: 978-0-9793562-1-6
      ISBN-10: 0-9793562-1-0

    1. Batting (Baseball) 2. Baseball for children—
Coaching. 3. Youth league baseball—Coaching.
I. Title.

GV869.P47 2009   796.357'26
                    QBI08-600257

To my wife Linda, my sons and daughter Matthew, Michal and Jackie.
I am so proud of all of you.
To kids of all ages — may your dreams come true.

Disclaimer

This book is meant to instruct coaches, parents and hitters. Caution should be exercised when performing the drills and swing suggestions associated with this book. The author and publisher accept no responsibility or liability in regard to any injury or loss that occurs directly or indirectly by performing any suggested material in this book. If you do not want to abide by this disclosure please return the book to the publisher for a full refund.

Contents

Foreword.. ix

Introduction xiii

1. Be the Coach You Were Meant to Be............................ 1
2. The Fundamentals.. 15
    Drill work... 38
    Five Drills to Teach the Fundamentals...................... 40
3. Instant Feedback 49
4. Having Fun 61
5. Advanced Hitting Drills..................................... 71
6. Teaching the Strike Zone 105
7. Coach Talk 109
8. Mental Side of Hitting..................................... 117
    Hitter's Agenda for a Good Mental Approach 124
9. Problem Solving.. 127
10. Other Hitting Topics 151
11. Developing the Hitter 171

Drills Summary... 176

Foreword

Hitting…The toughest thing to do in sports. You won't get much of an argument here! It also happens to be the toughest thing to *teach* in sports!

Early in my career the only thing I knew about hitting a baseball was that it was hard to do. As I started to understand my swing I could work on concepts to create drills to get a consistent swing. It wasn't always easy, but the first step of understanding my swing was critical. Every good hitter has an understanding of what makes their swing work and how to correct it when it is out of sync. One thing is certain…A hitter must keep it simple in preparation and maintenance to have a chance to be consistent.

I have known Jack Perconte for over 30 years and watched him become a terrific ballplayer through hard work. Jack, like most of us, had average physical talent but an incredible ability to learn from experience and incorporate changes into his game to make himself better.

This book is the best I've seen to help coaches (and dads like me) understand the swing and teach proper mechanics to help a young hitter reach his potential. Jack has broken it down better than anyone with concepts and drills that make this a must read for any coach, hitting instructor or baseball dad.

Teach your kids about their swings and have *fun* doing it…It's what baseball is all about!

— Mike Scioscia
L.A. Angels Manager

Acknowledgements

I would like to thank my family especially Mom, Dad, Jeanne and Marilyn — for the countless ways of always being there for me.

Thanks to:
The Rick Chignoli Family — great job Rob and Jimmy!
My nephews David and Sammy Wandolowski — looking good.

Thank you:
Nick Lewis and Doug Hafer at Publishers' Graphics, LLC — keep up the good work.
Rosa Lewis for all your hard work and time.
Mike Scioscia, an even better person than manager.
Thanks also to Ronda, Michele, Diane, Frank and the entire team at 1106 Design.

Thanks to all the great coaches I've had the pleasure to work with over the years. Finally, to all the young players I've had fun with for the past 19 years — thank you for the education.

Introduction

"I want you to make him a major leaguer"

"I just want her to have fun," or "he never wants to work at it," or "he won't listen to me, that's why we are here." These are all common requests I would get from parents who would bring their son or daughter in to one of our programs. All worthy requests but not really something I could make happen. Only the players themselves could make those things happen. However, I could show them the technique that could make them a major leaguer. I could make them feel better about themselves and that is usually fun. I could convince them that if they do A and B then the results will usually make them want to keep working at it. And finally, I could say things in a much more unemotional manner than mom or dad could and this usually would help, even if the parent was telling the hitter the same things.

Trying to figure out why a particular hitter isn't hitting is like a doctor trying to figure out what is wrong with his ill patient. First, they gather as much information about the illness as possible. Then using their experience and knowledge they analyze the symptoms to arrive at the prescription for the problem. This prescription may or may not work and if it doesn't, it is back to the doctor to try another remedy.

Since retiring from professional baseball in 1987, I have been playing the role of a doctor and sometimes a psychologist with hitters. I have worked with hitters of all ages over the past 19 years and I have given approximately 60,000 lessons. I'm sure that not all of my prescriptions have worked over the years but I have learned about a lot of symptoms and remedies over that time.

Even though I was fortunate to have played in the major leagues for a few years it was surprising how little I really knew about the fundamentals until I began to teach.

Just being able to do something doesn't automatically mean that you understand it and can teach it. I did feel qualified to teach though, because at one time or another I did about everything wrong fundamentally as a hitter. I can remember taking my bat back to the hotel with me to try and figure out what was going wrong. As the saying goes "I just wish I knew then what I know now." This book is an attempt to reveal the symptoms, remedies, and methods of teaching that I've learned about from teaching hitting.

For all parents and coaches, I hope to give you several ideas and methods for working with hitters that I have seen work well with players of all ages. For the less experienced coach, I hope to help you to understand hitting in order to help you guide your hitters in the future. For the more experienced coach, I hope to give you some insight as to how to deal with the hitter's faults as well as the mental side of hitting and teaching. Finally, for the serious hitter, there are some chapters that can give you a leg up on the competition.

This book isn't about different hitting theories, although some of the different ideas about hitting will be discussed from time to time. I still haven't developed what my philosophy of hitting is because every hitter brings a different "package" to the table so to speak. Every player brings different natural tendencies, strength levels, hitting knowledge and confidence levels to the plate. Each hitter has to be dealt with separately in order to get the proper swing out of them. At the same time the coach must help the hitter to develop the confidence in that swing for the hitter to be successful. The physical traits that a hitter has will often times determine what type of hitter they need to be and that determines what theory of hitting they need to learn. For instance, it doesn't make sense to teach a small fast player how to have a slightly upper cutting power swing. Just like it doesn't make sense to give a big powerful hitter a ground ball swing. So, with one hitter I would have to teach them one way of hitting and with the next hitter it seemed like I was teaching them some totally opposite things. Once again, all hitters have different habits so the coach must treat each a little differently.

No two players have the exact same swing and very few swings are problem free, especially with young hitters. Trying to get each hitter back to the basics is the challenge for the coach. Whenever you hear of a big league hitter getting out of a slump they always seem to say that they just simplified everything and went back to the basics. The basics can seem so simple to the observer (parent or fan), but making the necessary changes to the player's muscle memory can be very difficult. I always tried to keep things simple when teaching hitting, but once again it seemed like it was never really simple to get the hitter to just change their natural habits. Very rarely was it as simple as just telling the hitter to stop pulling his head out when a parent would come in and say that "he pulls his head out when he swings." There are so many things that can go wrong with a hitter's swing and it is not an easy task to be able to hit the ball consistently well.

I wish I had a dollar for every parent who said to me "My son is not hitting because it's in his head," or "my daughter has a great swing but she can't seem to make good contact" or "he hits every ball in practice, but never hits it in the game." If you find yourself saying this then this book can help. Pay particular attention to the "fundamentals" section of this book and the initial drills in that section. This should give your young player a good start towards understanding what needs to be done and developing the proper muscle memory to start putting the ball in play.

Furthermore, if you have a young aspiring player who loves the game and wants to improve and work hard but maybe doesn't know how to go about it, then this book should help. Start with "the fundamentals" section and proceed into the more advanced drills.

For the advanced hitter and coach this book will help you to figure out why a hitter is not making good contact and what to do to make the proper adjustments at home plate. When you are in a slump this book will be able to explain why you are getting the results you are getting and will suggest drills and ways of getting out of your slump. Simply look up the problem area and try the suggested solution drills.

Additionally, I tried to draw from my teaching experience to give you ways of becoming a trusted coach, friend and mentor to your child, student or team member.

Finally, for all hitters confidence is so important. This book will help you to develop a good mental approach which can go a long way to helping you become the best hitter you can be.

Here are a few more reasons why this book may be for you.

1. If you are a parent of a young ball player and want to help coach or have been asked to coach but are not sure you feel qualified then this book can be a great help.

2. If your son or daughter tells you to be quiet when you are trying to help them hit or they tune you out altogether, this book may help. Learn how to have better communication with your son, daughter or team and thus be able to enjoy your time together.

3. You can tell a hitter a thousand times what he is doing wrong but most of the time he will not be able to solve the problem until he puts in the

work and develops the correct muscle memory associated with hitting properly. Habits are hard to break. There are a variety of ideas and drills in this book that will help.

4. Just swinging a bat without hitting something is generally a boring exercise which most kids aren't going to do for long. If you really want players to work on hitting, give them the means, know how and fun associated with practice.

5. Even the great players have hitting coaches and are constantly analyzing and tweaking their swings. Just think of how much your son or daughter can improve with the proper know-how and coach. That coach can be you. Patience is mandatory though.

6. A hitter gets timing from a pitched ball, but he develops the proper swing from the drills and habits he develops in practice. Most hitting coaches will tell you that "hitters are not born they are made." This book can provide the drills that can make the difference in the player's development.

7. Remember, practice does not make perfect. "Perfect practice makes perfect."

It is better to take 10 fundamentally correct swings than to take 100 swings the wrong way. This book can help the coach understand what the perfect swing is to teach the hitter.

The information that follows is what I have learned over the last 19 years. I believe if you read the whole book you will find many insights into teaching hitting and becoming a better hitter. Although this book is geared towards the teaching of hitting, I believe there is much information that will help even the more experienced hitters. Sometimes, hitters are just one fundamental adjustment or thought process away from putting it all together. I hope they find it here.

1 | Be the Coach You Were Meant to Be

"It's not necessarily what you know, it's what you see"

1982 was a miserable year for me career wise. It was my first real shot at being an everyday player in the major leagues and the Cleveland Indians were giving me the opportunity. After a good spring training I lost confidence early in the season and just never recovered. During spring training the pitchers were pitching me inside and I was having success. From day one of the season the pitchers were pitching me away and I never did adjust. Confidence is so important to every athlete. Without it the athlete will play tentatively and scared of making mistakes. This usually leads to more mistakes. I know because I have been there many times.

Young players need to develop confidence and this is why the coaches and parents are so important. They can do this by creating an environment where it is OK for players to make mistakes as long as they learn from them. They should teach each player to believe in themselves. This will help the players build good self esteem and confidence. Finally, they should supply the fundamental knowledge that can help the players to be able to learn and adjust. This will give the players the opportunity to gain confidence.

When I began teaching hitters how to hit I was also learning myself. I realized that I lost confidence mainly because I didn't have the knowledge level necessary to make adjustments and thus I felt totally out of control. As I mentioned earlier, "if I only knew then what I know now."

When I say coach in this chapter or anywhere in this book for that matter, you can substitute the word parent also. In many ways the hitters' parents are their coach also. So it is important that the *parents learn how to communicate* with their child in the manner that they would like the coach to treat their son or daughter.

In the movie "Field of Dreams" you may recall the emotional feeling you had when the main character was able to play catch with his dad again. Or in the movie "City Slickers" when a character mentions the one thing his dad and he could always talk about was baseball. The bond that sports and baseball can create for your relationship is tremendous and everlasting. However, many relationships I've seen between the coach or parent and child become conflicted because of this emotional bond. Because the parent wants their own to succeed so badly they will actually make it more difficult for their child to succeed. Obviously, a parent will be tied up emotionally with their own child but it doesn't have to end up with tension between the two. I've often seen the pressure build up on players to the point where they want to quit playing or just end up playing only because the parent wants them to. Their love for playing is no longer there.

Working with your son or daughter at their skills should create a bond that will be a source of togetherness that can last a lifetime. Remember, if youngsters don't love playing and working on their game the chances of them playing into their high school years and possibly beyond are pretty much zero. By following the guidelines in this chapter and on the chapter about "Having Fun" I hope you can develop the bond between you and your child that will last a lifetime.

Many parents complain that their young ballplayer lacks the motivation to work on the game. If the game is not at all fun for the player then there is no amount of motivation tactics that will work. If they enjoy the game but still won't work on it, there is still hope. Don't push them into it and with time and some success they may come around and want to work on their skills. For the player who really enjoys playing then a good coach or parent can be a real motivator for the player. Whether the coach wants to be or not they are a role model for the young player. The players will always remember how you made them feel, so the coach needs to remember this when working with players. I know I can remember all the coaches I've ever had back to about seven years old. My first and best coach was my dad.

By following the guidelines in this section and on the "Having Fun" chapter in this book you can really make a difference in the player's future. The following is a list of the ingredients necessary to becoming the best coach you can be.

1. Knowledge of Hitting

There is obviously no substitute for understanding the fundamentals of hitting. As I mentioned in the introduction, just because a coach or parent was a good hitter when they played that doesn't automatically make them a proficient hitting instructor. Reading books like this one is a great place to learn. Watching video

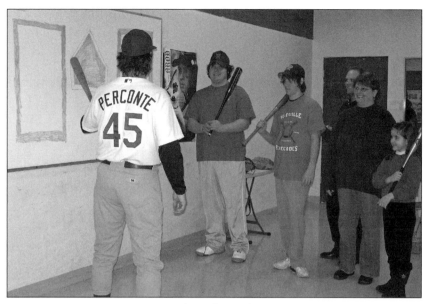

Explain the "Why"

of good hitters is another great way to learn the ins and outs of hitting. Talking to other coaches, asking questions and discussing hitting with others are all good ways to learn.

There are many coaches out there who can talk a good game but they *can't see* a good game. What is in books like this one is a great start but at some point the good coach will need to be able to pick up the little techniques in the swing that make the difference between success and failure. The way to do this is to observe hitters as much as possible. Watch them from as many angles as possible looking for the fundamentals or lack of them at each angle. The straight-on angle as when you are pitching to them, directly behind the hitter and the side view are all good for observing the hitter. These would be the best angles to film the hitters as well as for video analysis. Hang in there, and over time you will start to see the little intricacies of the hitter's swing.

As was mentioned earlier in this book, you can tell the hitter what they are doing wrong over and over again but that doesn't mean they will just be able to go up to the plate and correct it. The coach must give them ways (drills) to fix the problem areas.

2. Developing Trust

The first goal for the coach is attaining the hitters' trust in you as their coach. This is not always an easy task and involves more than just your knowledge of baseball.

It is an even tougher task if the student you are working with is your own child. Here are some keys to consider:

a) Wait

When you first begin to work with a hitter allow the hitter to fail for a little while — definitely don't start yelling or even commenting about how he should do this or that or "why" he isn't doing something when the hitter first begins to hit. Give the hitter some time to get the timing and to feel comfortable in the batter's box. However, the second you, the coach, see a good hit or even a good swing, jump on that and with an enthusiastic voice mention that to the hitter. "Good swing" or "nice hit" or "way to go" or "awesome" — anything that makes the hitter feel good about what they did and that shows them you are happy for them when they do something good. This will be the start of a good relationship where they know that they can make you happy when they do something the right way and where you didn't immediately start yelling instructions or any kind of negative feedback right away. The first few minutes together are the key. Once you feel like you have a grasp of what the hitter needs to work on then start with some positive words like, "That wasn't bad, now let's try this," or "Good job, I like the way you did such and such, now let's try this" or even "That was much better than last time, now let's move on to this" or "I can see you've been working on what we talked about last time, now let's try this." You get the idea: start with a positive especially referring to the good effort and then move on.

- ◆ I've seen so many hitting sessions begin with the coach (especially a parent) immediately starting to bark out instructions without allowing the student to miss a ball or two. Remember, wait for the good swing or good contact and *always mention this positive action first* in an encouraging and enthusiastic voice.

- ◆ I can remember back to my major league days where I have seen All Star caliber players come to spring training and miss every pitched ball for a day or two in batting practice. We would wonder if maybe they went blind over the off season only to see them begin to rip the cover off the ball in a day or two.

- ◆ Along the same line, *immediately after a game is not the time* to start telling a player or your child what he was doing wrong. Try to wait for a later time when the disappointment has worn off or it is a less emotional time — maybe after dinner that night or at practice the next day. If you start in on the player immediately after the game the player may not look forward to games or to you being there to see them maybe fail. Remember, wait and you will begin to gain the player's trust and enjoy each other's time together much more.

b) How and What to Say

A strong trust between you the coach and your player will be developed if you learn to give advice in a positive way. First, use a matter-of-fact voice when giving advice and your emotional voice only on good hits or good improvement. Second, try to describe the action and not the player. Things like "Your swing was not there today" or "your timing was off a little" or "It was just one of those days" are much better than saying "You are never going to hit like that" or "You better go home and start practicing tonight" or the worst "I'm not going to keep paying for you to play if you are going to do that." Third, stay optimistic and encouraging — it won't happen over night.

c) Give the Why for What You Ask the Hitter to Do

It is also important to give the reason why you want the player to try something new or why you want him to work on a certain drill. The hitter may not fully comprehend the why but when they see some better results after trying it they will understand more. Keep the "why" simple. A demonstration of the drill by you or another player is helpful. Some kids are more visual learners so a lengthy verbal explanation isn't necessary and showing them the correct way is a great teaching tool.

Be careful of embarrassing yourself though — it may not be as easy as it once was for you — I've see many a parent hop in the batting cage to show their son or daughter how to do it only to fail miserably. (It will give everybody else a good chuckle though.)

d) We

If you are the coach or parent tell the player that "we will get it" as if you are a team and it is not just him or her. To expect the hitter to be able to figure out hitting and make the changes necessary on their own *can be an overwhelming feeling* for the young player. I never could figure it out even though I played at the major league level until I learned to by teaching and studying it. Tell the hitter that the two of you will figure it out in time and both will leave with a *smile* on their faces.

3. PATIENCE

This is the third key to good coaching. A good coach (parent) realizes that it is very difficult to excel at hitting or any skill for that matter. They also realize that just because something is easy for them or for some doesn't mean that it will be easy for everyone. However, a good coach also realizes that each player who really cares to improve has the ability to improve if they are willing to work at it. I have been amazed by the improvement of some hitters who I thought were beyond hope. Any player who is willing to work on it is not a waste of time for the coach.

A good coach further realizes that it is not usually enough to tell a player what they are doing wrong and then assume that the player can just go out and correct the problem. As mentioned earlier, you can tell a player something a thousand times and their muscle memory will not let them change a certain habit. The hitter will need to perform the correct habit the thousand times or so in order to create a new habit and overcome the problem. Obviously, this takes time so it is important that the coach has a great amount of patience and understands that the player is usually trying, but their *muscle memory will not change* over night. Other ideas to consider are the following:

a) Remember, each player has a different personality and attitude. Be patient with each player. Many players can fool you with their initial demeanor as they give off an "I don't care attitude." I found that many times they do care and like the game. It is simply their way at first. However, be careful of the player who likes to "screw around" and bring others along with them. Try to pull this player aside and explain that there is a fine line between having fun and messing around. When the messing around begins to affect the amount and quality of work getting done then the player needs to be dealt with. If the disruptive player has what seems to be a good relationship with their parents, then mention the player's behavior to them. If it doesn't seem like the relationship with his parents is sound, then you are better off not mentioning it, and this player may come around just because you didn't talk to them about it. This is a tough area, but patience and understanding will help.

b) Set longer-range goals for the hitter. Instead of saying by next game or even next week tell the player that "we" can have it solved in a month (a minor problem) or by the end of the season (a more ingrained habit) or even by the time the player reaches high school (a major overhaul or a very inexperienced player). Each player develops at a different rate, so *expect setbacks or plateaus* for a period before improvement is shown.

c) It is easier to create new muscle memory with drills on a tee or with drops or short flips as opposed to trying to solve a bad habit with a pitched ball. Remember, batting practice is generally for timing and not necessarily for breaking bad habits. Find the specific drill that most helps the hitter overcome the problem and have him focus on that for a long period of time — remember, practice doesn't make perfect; rather, "perfect practice makes perfect."

d) Stay encouraging and positive and remember that even big leaguers have some "holes" in their swings and they work on it all the time.

e) Avoid the "looks of disgust" or the "quick negative retort" or the "look away" when the player does not do something correctly or isn't improving at the rate you want him to. These gestures will only make the hitter feel more pressure and give them the feeling that they are letting you down. With time these gestures may even make them want to give up working at it or even playing at all.

f) Coaches who show patience with their players develop patient hitters who won't mind working on their skills, realizing that they will improve in time.

Many of these topics will be discussed when you get to the "Having Fun" chapter in this book.

4. Homework

Yes, the dreaded "h" word. A good coach will give the student something to work on or something to think about when they leave practice. There is generally not enough time for the coach to solve major problems for each player at practice so homework is important.

a) Try to involve the parent if possible and let them know what you want the player working on. The exception to this would be if you notice a parent is hard on their child and puts a lot of pressure on their son or daughter. Then it is better to just let the youngster know what you want them to be working on.

b) Each player has different habits so different homework drills may be necessary for different players. However, you usually can not go wrong with the fundamental drills found in the chapter on teaching the fundamentals.

c) Having kids watch baseball or find pictures of hitters are always good assignments too.

d) Obviously, you won't know if the players do their homework or not, but at least you will have done your job. Ask your players at the next practice who did their homework — even if only a few did it, that can sometimes spur the others to do it the next time.

Assume Nothing.

5. Challenge

A good coach will challenge his hitters according to their own skill level.

a) If working with a team, a good coach must recognize the different skill levels of each player and begin to challenge each differently. If not on the first day then soon after. Explain to the players that you will be challenging each one of them a little differently in the future.

b) Changing speeds and locations of pitches are great ways of challenging the hitters.

c) The key is to challenge the player up to the point where frustration is about to set in and then back off. When you sense the players are beginning to get frustrated, back off and try to get their minds away from what they are doing. This can be done by asking them a question about something else or about a game you might have seen, etc.

d) Your objective is avoiding boredom, and challenging the players will help. I've seen many good players stop playing because of boredom from not being challenged properly. Obviously, the weaker players need more work, but don't forget the more advanced player and divide your time equally. The more advanced drills in this book will be a good start with the advanced players.

e) I've see many players, even young ones, who learn to make adjustments at the plate on their own if they are consistently challenged. The coach or parent does not even have to be yelling out instructions.

Coaching Tip — Positive Motivation

There may come a time when the coach does have to "come down" on the team for the apparent lack of effort or bad attitudes. This is OK as long as it is based on these reasons and not on the failure to win. Coaches may have to raise their voices and express their displeasure with the team's effort. This should be done in a productive way. Express to the players that they can only control the input and not always the results. The coach should emphasize that if they continue to work hard and stay positive, better results will come. The coach should tell them of the importance of staying positive and pulling for each other. Remember, the coach is the role model, and how the *coach handles tough times* will be how the team reacts. Stay positive and let your team know that you won't allow them to stop working and you won't accept negative thoughts.

It only takes a player or two to bring down the attitude of the whole team. If this is the case, take the negative players aside and talk to them individually. *Don't penalize* the whole group for the actions of a few.

Coaching Tip — Are They Listening?

All coaches want to believe that their players are listening to every word they say. Obviously, they are not and it is important to understand that the average attention span for players (especially young ones) is not that long. The best way to find out if the players are listening is to ask questions. This is a good way to begin and end practices. I've been fooled many times as to which players were listening and which were not. Just because a player is not looking at you doesn't mean he is not listening. The ones who are looking at you may be wondering why you look so mad and have no idea what you are talking about. The only way to know is to ask questions. Try not to show any particular player up, but letting the players know that they may be called upon to answer a question will put a little pressure on them to try to pay more attention.

6. Develop Aggressive Hitters

First of all let's define what an aggressive hitter is:
   a) Aggressive hitters go to home plate not afraid to swing the bat.
   b) Aggressive hitters are expecting the next pitch to be the ideal pitch for them to hit and are ready for it. They think "swing" until the last possible second when they may hold up if the pitch isn't their pitch.
   c) Aggressive hitters want to be the hitter with runners on base.
   d) Aggressive hitters want to be the hitter with the game on the line in the last inning.

What the coach can do to teach this type of aggressiveness:

    a) Not get upset when the hitter swings at bad pitches.

    b) Teach the hitters what pitches are best suited for their particular swing and have them ready for that pitch on every pitch.

    c) In practice put the hitters in game situations with players on base as much as possible. The coach should teach the different game situations that may occur and how to handle these situations. Knowing which situations to be more aggressive in and when to be more patient. See below.

    d) Along the same line, put the hitters in game winning situations during batting practice as much as possible so when the situation occurs in a game they will have "been there" many times before.

    e) Teaching the hitters a fearless attitude by not dwelling on the outs that the hitter makes is the most important thing the coach can do to keep the hitters' aggressiveness. (Many of these topics will be discussed in upcoming chapters in this book.)

7. Developing Intelligent Hitters

One of the coach's jobs is to teach the players situational hitting. This means that a particular situation in the game calls for the hitter to perform a task besides just hitting. This is a developmental process that sometimes takes players years to learn. Oftentimes the coaches of young players don't understand game situations enough to help the hitters either. I will try to cover some of these situations and thought processes that can be taught. Even hitters in the major leagues have to be reminded of what to do in certain situations, and as a coach you should never take for granted that a player knows what to do.

For curious and more advanced players, there is no age that is too young to teach some of these situational hitting ideas, although players below the age of ten should just concentrate on hitting the ball in games. They should not be asked to do the following. How to perform the following tasks will be discussed later in this book:

    a) Take Sign – This is when the coach gives a sign to the hitter not to swing at the next pitch no matter where it is pitched. I believe it is OK to play to win but this sign should only be used on 3 and 0 counts late in the game for ages ten and above. I feel that is the only count on which the take sign should be used for players up until the high school varsity level. Using the take sign at other times does not allow the hitter to ever learn the strike zone on their own. The take sign may hurt players' confidence and give them the attitude that getting a walk is what their objective is. Remember, it is the coach's responsibility to develop hitters and not pitch takers.

b) Bunting – The coach should stress the importance of the bunting game, especially to sacrifice runners up a base. Don't abuse the bunt by having certain players bunt almost every time up to bat, though. Only use if the situation absolutely calls for a bunt. All hitters at the high school level should be able to bunt. At the higher levels the coach may ask the hitter to not only bunt but to lay the bunt down in a particular direction.

c) Hit and Run – The hit and run is a play where the base runner is running on the pitch and the hitter is required to swing and try to hit a ground ball. This is usually not used till ages thirteen and above. There are many situations where this may be used, but usually it is to stay out of the double play or to try to create some action in the game.

d) Runner on Second – Advance the Runner – Generally, for advanced baseball this is used to get the runner over to third base with no outs. The coach does not want to bunt, so they are depending on the hitter hitting the ball to the right side of the field in order to advance the runner.

e) Hitting a Sacrifice Fly – With a runner on third base and less than two outs, the team has a good chance of scoring the run if the ball is hit to the outfield. The coach should teach the hitter not to uppercut but to look for a pitch that they can get in the air and drive it to the outfield.

f) Runners in Scoring Position – It is hard to knock in runs without contact. So it's important to teach the hitters the necessity of being more aggressive with runners in scoring position. The hitters in this situation need to be swinging earlier in the at-bat in order to put the ball in play. As the level of play increases and the pitchers get more accomplished, the hitter does not want to have two strikes on them too often in this situation and thus be forced to have to swing at the pitcher's pitch.

g) Squeeze Bunt – This is where the runner on third will break for home, and the hitter has to bunt the ball on the ground, or the runner will probably be out at home. The coach at the younger levels should only use this to win a game and must teach the play correctly or it can be a very dangerous play.

These are the main situational hitting plays that a good coach will teach. With time the good players will start to know on their own what the situation calls for. Again, how to perform these actions will be covered in the "Other Hitting Topics" chapter.

8. Dealing with Parents

Anyone who has coached before knows that this is one of the most important aspects of coaching. If all goes well with the parents of your players, the season will go smoothly and your sanity will remain intact. Even coaches who have the best intentions can run into problems. Many of the confrontations that occur between the coach and the parent can be averted if the coach goes about it the right way. In my opinion, the key to the parent and coach relationship is the preseason meeting with all the parents and coaches. Make this a mandatory meeting and encourage both parents to attend. Let the parents know in the invitation that you will not be happy about discussing things later in the season that were discussed at the meeting if they didn't attend it in the first place. Try to address the important issues that usually cause friction as the season progresses. Here are some sample guidelines for things that should be discussed at the opening season meeting. Notice I said discussed — try not to make it a monologue but a discussion where parents feel free to ask questions and provide input.

a) Give the parents some background information about all the coaches, especially about their background with regard to the particular sport that they are coaching. Be honest about your coaching experience.

b) Express your philosophy of coaching. The three objectives of coaching are winning, player development and fun. What percentage do you plan on attributing to each objective? I would suggest a 30, 30 and 30 split saving the extra 10 percent for the area needed most. This 10 percent will depend on the overall competitiveness of the team. The coach may have a different philosophy depending on the level and competitiveness of the competition. State clearly though what the plans are at this first meeting so there is no mistaking the goals later on. Maybe I'm old school but I believe that it is OK to play to win even at the young level, as long as it is kept in perspective.

c) Along the same lines, discuss your philosophy of playing time, batting order and positions played. Once again, let the parents know how you plan to run the team. For example, do the players have to earn their position on the field or in the batting order, or will you naturally rotate the players, etc.? Talk over any issues that the parents or coaches may have. Be sure to recognize and discuss the objectives of the league and level that the team is playing at.

d) Discuss when and *how the coaches can be approached during the season* so that it is in a non-confrontational way. Set up a system where this conversation is away from the players, other parents and crowds. There will be issues that pop up from time to time, but let the parents know that even though there are disagreements things can be handled in a civil way away from the young players.

You get the idea. Discuss any likely issues before they occur and many problems can be averted. Be sure to tell the parents to share the coaches' philosophies with their child so they understand the coaches' plans also. Most of the time, the players are pretty *happy with playing* and being around their new and old friends. Things start to change when the parents start to mumble and grumble at home to the players about the coach. Insist to the parents that they approach you first before getting too upset and spoiling the fun for their child. There are some good books out in the book stores that deal with this area more in depth.

Most issues arise because the players and parents do not feel the coach is being fair. *It is important that the coach lives up to the philosophy statement* made at the beginning of the season meeting. If the coaches are out to win and this is a major emphasis, then state this at the beginning. Problems will occur if the coach or coaches change their philosophy midseason.

Once again, I believe it is OK to play to win. This will provide great *teaching moments* for parents and coaches to help young players learn to deal with winning and losing. Sportsmanship is sometimes forgotten in this era, but it should be taught at a young age. Once again, the coaches and parents should always keep in mind the level and objectives of the particular league that the team is competing in.

▶ *Final Thought* ◀

Remember, hitters are made. They can develop a great swing and learn good plate discipline. Along the same line coaches are also made. Coaches can develop a great relationship with their players. They should be a role model and communicator of information to their players.

2 | The Fundamentals

"Fundamentals are fundamentals — they don't change
for the big leaguer or the little leaguer"

I was not very big growing up, so baseball was a sport that I had a chance to compete at. As a freshman in high school, I only weighed about 100 pounds. I remember telling a friend one day that I hoped to become a major league baseball player. He laughed so hard that I never told another person that that was my goal. That is one of the great things about baseball — size doesn't matter. Of course it is not an easy game to keep advancing levels in because it requires some abilities that are "God given," so to speak. I was blessed with good hand-eye coordination, very good eye sight and quickness. I was amazed when I got to professional baseball with how big and fast players were. I thought I was a fast runner till players much bigger than me were running right past me. When growing up, lifting weights were not recommended for baseball players. Luckily, lifting became popular around the time I entered college, and this helped me to be able to compete at the higher levels.

Many athletes have similar abilities, gifts and desires as I had. Why some players make it and others don't is a combination of things. First, there is always an amount of luck that goes into anything. Sure, people who work the hardest may have more luck but luck is still involved. Second, it takes someone who really believes in the player and is a catalyst for their career and goal. Finally, it requires a great fundamental base that the player can fall back on in order to repeat the required actions on a consistent basis. This chapter is about understanding the fundamentals that are required to advance the player's career and "keep the dream alive."

The mental game and the ability to focus are very important aspects of hitting. However, neither of those is of much use without the good, sound fundamentals necessary to perform well. The good players are able to repeat the same actions over and over again in game situations. The difference between the Triple A player and the big league player is this consistency of action. This is the reason why a player may get cut from his high school team over another player of equal ability. The coach feels like the one player can repeat the necessary actions more consistently.

Hitting is often talked about as being the toughest skill in all of sports. I don't know if that is true, but I do know that if there is any little flaw in the hitter's mechanics then it will show up in the inability to hit the ball solidly. It doesn't always show up immediately but it will as the player advances levels. Many times my nerves were eased in an at-bat or game because my swing was just right and line drives just happened. Give me a great swing and I'll take my chances with being nervous at the plate.

I've often heard coaches and people around the game say that there is "no one way of getting the job done." This may be true to some extent, but when it comes to hitting there are certain fundamentals that need to be performed correctly if the hitter is to have success. There is just no way around certain fundamentals if the player is to keep advancing levels and having success. There are different "styles" and looks especially with a player's initial setup and stance, but when it comes time to swing the bat, certain positions and moves must be made in order to hit the ball squarely on a consistent basis.

One of the biggest concerns I would receive from parents over the years was that their child takes his eye off the ball when he swings. It was as if the hitter was purposely taking his eye off of the ball when he was about to hit it. I have never known a hitter to want to take his eye off the ball. But the mechanics of his swing would cause his head to pull and thus take his eye off the ball. When hitters use the big muscles of the arms and shoulders too much and not enough hands and hips, then this is why the head pulls. Hitters need to learn how to use the right muscles and the right fundamentals to keep their eye on the ball. If hitters use the hands and hips correctly, they will keep their eye on the ball. This is up to the coach to help the players with.

◆   ◆   ◆

Before getting to the fundamentals, it is important to understand that starting position (the hitter's set up before the stride) and hitting position (the point from which we actually start our swing forward) are two different things. Each hitter has their own "style" when it comes to getting in the box and getting setup. Some have a narrow stance with their bat flat, whereas some have a wider stance and their bat straight up, etc. It is also important to understand that the setup position is not what is important — each individual's style is their own, and I don't like to mess with that very much. The *hitting position* that the hitter arrives at when the front foot lands (post stride) is what is important. The correct position at this point is mandatory for becoming an accomplished hitter. If a hitter can begin out of "hitting position" and arrive in the proper position at front foot landing then that is fine.

Having said this, I have found that most young hitters cannot start out of hitting position and than proceed to the proper position. Many young players try to mimic the hitting style of a certain big league ball player, failing to realize that style and good fundamentals are different. There are great players who have unorthodox setups but always have good, sound fundamental actions when it comes time to swing the bat. It's difficult for the young player to start with an unorthodox setup and then go to the correct hitting actions that the big league player can perform. Thus, I would usually try to get them to start in the correct "hitting position" so there is less room for error. The older, more accomplished hitters generally can learn to go from an incorrect setup and move to the correct hitting position. Remember, the key to hitting is that we arrive at the correct hitting position in time to swing the bat and that is all that matters. What the hitter does before this point is OK and their individual style. I've found that many coaches and parents get upset when their hitters are waving the bat or appear to be dancing around before the ball is pitched. This is OK and usually is just some nervous energy. This movement can be good, for things in motion will usually be quicker and more explosive than static positions. This movement from incorrect hitting position to the correct position is what we call a "trigger" movement. The correct hitting position and the "trigger" will be explained below.

I cannot emphasize enough that it is OK for a hitter to start wrong and go to the right position. Obviously, it is also OK for the hitter to start with the right position and maintain this position as the pitch is approaching home plate. Sometimes we get fooled by hitters who start in the correct hitting position but then lose this position when they take their stride. A majority of young hitters do not get into the right hitting position or maintain it when the ball is coming toward them and thus limit their chance of becoming a good hitter. This flaw of not getting to the correct hitting position may not always show with negative results at a young age but *always* will show up when the player reaches a higher level, especially when curve balls and change ups come into play.

It takes a keen and trained eye to notice the little imperfections in a player's "hit position" and "swing." Unfortunately, it only takes a little flaw to cause a major slump or to cause a hitter to be unable to make solid contact. Even if the coach cannot pick up on these little hitting imperfections in your player's swing, this book can give you the drills to eliminate the problem areas.

Finally, the younger the hitter, the easier it should be to break or form new habits. So it is never too young to begin to teach the correct fundamentals. Usually, at about 7 years old a youngster can start to comprehend the basics of hitting. The obvious drawback to the younger hitter picking up the right fundamentals, though, is the strength factor. Many young players are not physically strong enough, especially with their hands and forearms, to hit correctly. Try not to stop teaching the correct fundamentals though, because the young one will get stronger with growth and age. When the hitters do reach the strength level necessary, they will have a good understanding and basis for turning into a very good hitter.

The older the hitter the more ingrained are most of their habits. I found it much harder to change the mechanics of the older hitter's swing. The older hitters have the advantage of being stronger so they can overcome their hitting problems with good concentration and repetition. This is not easy, though, because the muscle memory is so set that it takes a great amount of work to overcome. The incorrect habits one develops at a young age will be very hard to break if they are not caught soon enough. We all remember the little league star who was bigger and better than everyone at that level only to have stopped playing before reaching high school. They were good athletes and bigger than everyone else but not fundamentally sound. For the smaller sized player out there, do not give up. Keep working on the good fundamentals and some day you will grow up and out play many of the big boys. I was one of those smaller sized players.

Teaching The Fundamentals

1. Bat Size
Most Common Problem – Bat Too Long
Coaching Tip – "Light but right, and not too long"

Most aluminum bats made nowadays are pretty light, and I don't believe an ounce or two makes a difference in one's swing. Having said that, I don't believe in the use of the big barreled bat for players less than 12 years of age. Unless the player is on the big and strong side, most players less than twelve will struggle with the bigger barrel.

However, I do believe that the *length of the bat* is very important for most hitters. Many hitters grab a bat that is too long for them and sometimes too short and this definitely will affect their mechanics of hitting. I usually go by age to help a hitter determine the proper length. Below is a general guideline for most hitters (not taking into account the size of the particular athlete). You can add or subtract an inch for exceptionally big or small players. It's always a good idea to check with your league regulations for bat sizes before buying a bat. I've seen many a parent spend a lot of money on a bat only to find out later that it is not legal for the particular league.

Age	Bat Size
Under seven	Tee Ball Bat
seven	27"
eight	28"
nine & ten	28" or 29"
eleven	29" or 30"
twelve	30" or 31"
thirteen & fourteen	31" or 32" big barrel minus 7 or 5*
High School	
Freshman & Sophomore	32" minus 3
Varsity	33" minus 3

* The minus refers to the difference between the length of the bat and the ounces of the bat.

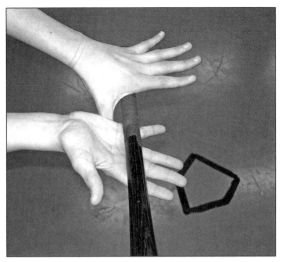

Grip must be correct for the correct hand position at contact.

2. The Grip
Most Common Problem – Setting the bat too deep in the hands and having to squeeze it too tight.
Coaching Tip – "Relax the hands and forearms"

An incorrect grip will cause the incorrect position of the hands at contact. This will affect the ability to hit the ball hard and consistently. With this in mind I like to check the hitter's grip at contact position. While holding the bat, I have the hitters put their hands into the right position of the bat at contact. From this position check to see if the palms are aligned correctly. The palm of the bottom hand should be parallel to the ground and the top hand should be parallel to the sky, with the hands exactly parallel to each other. When the hands are exactly parallel then have the hitter grab the bat in that position and maintain it when bringing it back to the setup position. You should find that the bat is now sitting in the upper palm just below the start of the fingers. I usually don't try to line up any of the knuckle lines as all hand sizes are different.

This method will also serve the purpose of teaching how the hands and arms are positioned when contact is made with the ball.

3. Plate Positioning
Most Common Problem – Lack of plate coverage
Coaching Tip – "Make sure you can cover the outer half of home plate"

This is very important because the wrong distance from home plate will usually cause the wrong swing direction. The most common strategy would be to have the hitter be able to touch the end of the bat one inch past the outside corner while holding the bat with the hand closest to the pitcher. Have the hitter bend the knees slightly and lean forward with the head. Keeping the knees bent slightly and the head forward, have the hitter set up to face the pitcher, maintaining his weight slightly forward on the balls of his feet. Hitters who stand too far from or too close to home will have to alter the correct fundamentals of hitting to hit the ball.

4. Feet Alignment
Most Common Problem – Stance too closed
Coaching Tip – "Stay square so you can see the ball and be able to square the hips when swinging."

Ideally, it is best to keep the hitters with an even stance. This means each foot is the same distance away from home plate and on a direct line parallel to the pitcher. A little open or closed with the feet is OK, but the hitter should try to avoid the much closed or very open stance. The distance the feet are apart is personal preference but balance is important in the setup. A closed stance means that the foot closest to the pitcher is closer to the plate than the rear foot. The open stance is the opposite, where the back foot is closer to the plate than the front foot. An even stance will allow the hitter to see the pitcher's release point with both eyes while still maintaining a good fundamental position.

The most common position in the batter's box would be to set the lead foot at the point where the plate breaks back to the tip.

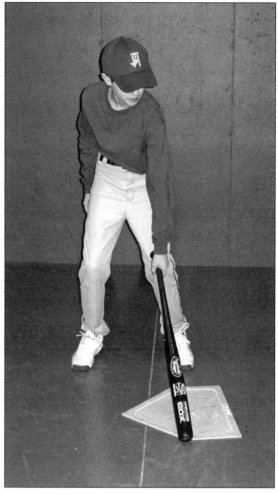

Correct plate coverage can prevent possible swing problems from developing.

A square stance allows good vision
of the ball and less stride issues.

Too closed stance — may prevent good vision
and leads to stride direction problems.

Open stance — OK but stride back in must be correct.

5. Balance
Most Common Problem – Flat
footed hitters
*Coaching Tip – "Keep your weight
on the balls of the feet"*

The best way to find the ideal balance position is to have the hitters jump as high as they can. The hitter should freeze upon landing and maintain that position. They will not usually land flat footed, so this will work to help them understand their ideal balance position. Obviously, this is not something they will do when they get in the batter's box but is a good teaching tool for young hitters who have a hard time understanding where the balls of their feet are and what balance means. (Also, kids will have fun jumping.)

Another way of checking balance is to go up to the hitters in their stance and try to push them in each direction. If you can move them in a certain direction very easily then they are probably not well balanced to begin with. This is a good way to get hitters off their heels in their stances. For the players who are very serious about baseball, the use of a balance beam as described in the advanced drill chapter of this book is invaluable.

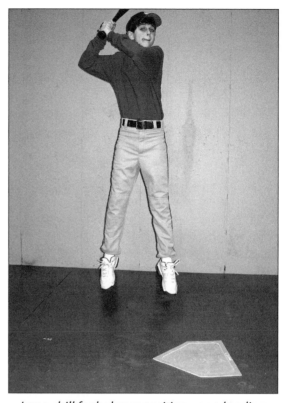

Jump drill for balance position upon landing.

Balance.

Balance.

Balance.

6. Upper Body and Bat Starting Position

Most Common Problem – Starting their hands too far from hitting position

Coaching Tip – "A hitter is stronger when things (hands and bat) are close to us"

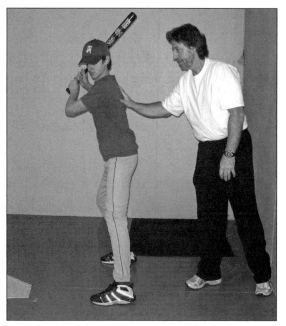

Balance.

The younger the hitter the more important it is to have the hitter start in the ideal hitting position. The bat should be positioned with the top hand even with the top of the shoulder. The hands should be an open hand's distance away from the shoulder and an inch or two back of the shoulder. The front elbow should be down and pointed to the front of home plate. The back elbow should be in a comfortable position but *closer* to the catcher than the hands are to the catcher. There is merit to keeping the back elbow up as long as the elbow remains comfortable and no higher than the back shoulder level. Sometimes terminology and perception get in the way of understanding about the position of the back elbow. What is an "up" elbow to some is not to others. Like I said above I like the hitter to keep the elbow outside the hands, but how far up is personal preference and comfort level. This will ensure that the

Open hand's distance from shoulder — inch or two back of shoulder.

swing doesn't become a long stiff arm swing. Keeping the back elbow beyond the hands will force the hitters to use their hands and forearms when they swing.

This is difficult for young hitters who have not developed hand and forearm strength yet. Because the young hitter will feel much stronger with their arms up and away from their body, they tend to hit this way. This problem will surface at some point because the longer arm swing will not allow them to be able to hit certain pitches. When the competition level increases this arm swing will make it much tougher to hit the ball solidly.

Check to make sure the hitter's lead forearm is parallel to the ground and the hitter's head is upright with the eyes level. This position should mean that the hitter's shoulders are also level at startup. The angle of the bat should be so that the knob of the bat is pointing down and slightly back towards the catcher's feet. The trademark of the bat is on a line directly above the hitter's back shoulder. This bat position is another one of the keys to giving the hitter a chance to be a good hitter. The *swing will begin with a slight pull* of the lead hand. If the knob of the bat is not down at this point then the lead elbow will jut out on the initial move, causing the hands and bat to start on an incorrect line to the ball.

The player's head should be turned, level and with both eyes being able to focus on the pitcher's release point.

♦ There are a very few hitters who are successful with the bat in a position where the trademark is not angled directly above the back shoulder line. I would see the most consistent contact with the bat barrel directly above

Good bat position — notice the box or rectangle.

the shoulder line. Make sure the hitter is not allowing the bat to "wrap" around their head. This wrapping action is when the bat barrel can be seen behind the hitter's back and on the pitcher's side of the hitter's head. This creates a longer swing which is more difficult to hit from. The knob of the bat should point *down* towards the catcher's feet and not towards the catcher's head or body.

Back & ready. Good job, Jimmy.

◆ This hitting position of the arms is often referred to as a box. If set up correctly there is a rectangle formed — the lead forearm is one side, with the bat a side, the shoulders a side and the front upper arm the final side (see illustration). The ability to maintain or go to this rectangular position before swinging is another way of thinking about the correct hitting position.

◆ This starting position is so important to developing a *compact swing* and being able to get to the correct contact position as soon as possible. Every inch that the bat is out of correct starting position will put the point of arm extension at contact out in front of home at least an extra half foot or more. The failure to start correctly is detrimental to being able to get the barrel to certain pitches. All good hitters who start out of the correct hitting position will arrive at the correct position when their front foot lands, or before. Additionally, they will begin the swing from the position that all good hitters do, regardless of their initial set up.

7. Trigger (Preparation)
Most Common Problem – No movement to prepare to swing
Coaching Tip – "Don't be a statue – get ready"

I always found this action one of the toughest aspects of hitting fundamentals to teach. It was like some hitters did it naturally, and for the ones who didn't, it was difficult to develop the trigger action without having to think about it. If the hitter has to

Getting prepared — "don't be a statue."

think about triggering and take his mind off the ball, it is not good. Immediately before the stride is taken, about the time the pitcher begins his movement towards home plate, the hitter will begin a slight backwards movement to prepare the bat and body to swing. This "cocking" or "loading" action slightly back towards the catcher can come from the upper body (front shoulder) or lower body (front knee tuck). If the loading action is done with the lower body knee tuck, the hitter's front shoulder will automatically close a little also. This is a great way to prepare the whole body. If the load just comes from the front shoulder the hitter will need to begin with more weight on the back leg.

The hitter's grip and upper body should still be relaxed and as tension-free as possible with this trigger action. It is essential that this action is done on time while still maintaining a good balanced hitting position. This action will also get the hitter's *weight back* on the leg closest to the catcher, which is important for proper preparation and for allowing a proper weight *shift and power* to the swing. Be careful that the hitter does not over turn and have his whole back facing the pitcher, which can cause a big problem. Also, make sure the hitter's weight and head do not move beyond the back foot to where the hitter's weight gets to the outside of the back foot. The timing of all this is essential and takes a lot of practice to make it natural. There will be some timing and rhythm drills in the advanced drills section that can help with this loading action.

8. Stride (Step towards Pitcher)
Most Common Problem – Stepping out
Coaching Tip – "Soft, controlled stride towards the pitcher"
Having the hitter begin with a balanced stance as found in Fundamental 5 is the key to a controlled stride. It is difficult to over-stride from this balanced starting position. The first thing that should land with the stride is the ball of the front foot up near the

toes. This will help insure that the weight is remaining back with the stride. The whole foot will land immediately after. It is important that the hitter learns to stride with the head staying back. This will also keep the weight on the back side. Staying closed on the front side is important. This means that the hitter's hips and shoulder do not open towards the pitcher with the stride.

Ball of foot landing, then the whole foot.

The direction of the stride is another story and very important. The hitter should step towards the pitcher on the parallel line that was begun with the even stance.

◆   ◆   ◆

Ideally, the stride is the *same* on every pitch. It does not change for inside and outside pitches. The stride will start at about the pitcher's release point but the swing will not start till the ball arrives. So when the stride is taken the hitter will not know the location of the pitch yet. Keeping the front toe from opening is essential for keeping the hips closed and thus not losing power. For some hitters it is natural for the front foot to open slightly when striding, and this is acceptable as long as the hips and hands do not come forward. Landing on the ball (up near the toes) of the front foot will usually mean that the front side is remaining closed. It is difficult to land on the ball of the foot and open the foot. If the hitter's front foot opens too much, they are usually landing on the whole foot or on their heels, and this is incorrect.

9. Hitting Position
Most Common Problem – Losing control of the bat barrel
Coaching Tip – "Feel the barrel at all times."

Once again, this is the key time for hitters. It is mandatory that they are in the correct position to swing the bat when the ball arrives. The keys to this are the following:

a) The hitter's feet are parallel to home plate with a controlled stride towards the pitcher. The stride should come from the lead leg without the head moving forward.

Good job, Rob. Weight and hands back, hip and shoulder closed at foot strike.

b) The shoulders remain level with the hands staying up and back an inch or two beyond the back shoulder.

c) The hitter maintains good balance, with the head as the key. The head should be level, remaining back, on the same plane and slightly towards home plate. On the same plane means that the head is not going up or down with the stride.

d) The correct bat angle when the foot lands is crucial to becoming a good hitter. (Knob down and angled back towards the catcher's feet with the trademark on a line directly above the back shoulder.)

e) The front foot should be landing as the ball is just getting to the hitter It is at this point that the hitter must decide to swing or not. The weight is still on the back leg at this point but ready to shift forward.

Many hitters will hit from this incorrect position.

10. First Move (Beginning of Swing)

Most Common Problem – Allowing the lead elbow to rise up (Chicken Wing)

Coaching Tip – "Use the hands to swing the bat"

At this point the back knee will begin to break in towards the pitcher and the hands will begin forward, maintaining the knob at a downward angle. As mentioned earlier this action will begin with a slight pulling action from the lead hand. Keeping the front elbow from flying up is the key here. The back elbow will begin down also and will remain *close* to the body on this first move. The back elbow should never have to get away from the body unless the hitter is swinging at a pitch over his hands (on a hit and run for instance). With the same thought, the hands will remain close to the body on the initial portion of the swing also. On the outside pitch the hands will begin on the same path and then move away somewhat as the swing occurs. This is known as an inside-out swing. Keep in mind that all good swings come from the inside of the ball in order to get to the correct contact position. This is what is meant by the phrase "stay inside the ball."

First move begins with back knee break with knob of bat and front elbow remaining down.

11. Swing Plane

Most Common Problem – Barrel leveling off behind the hitter

Coaching Tip – "Gradually level the bat off"

As mentioned above, maintaining the knob of the bat down will start the bat on a direct angle towards the pitched ball. The bat will level off sooner on lower pitches than on higher pitches. On all pitches the bat is usually level by the time the barrel reaches the rear hip. With the hips continuing to open towards the ball the bat will come forward as if landing an airplane with the goal of meeting the ball in the palm-up, palm-down position mentioned earlier (see Fundamental 2). It is this "contact" positioning of the hands that levels off the swing and allows us to hit the balls to all fields with authority.

◆ There is an ongoing debate as to whether the swing is down, level or slightly up. The swing involves all three and the proper sequence of these is important. The bat head should begin with a downward movement towards the ball and the strike zone. It gradually levels off and remains level through the hitting zone at which time the bat will begin an upward arc till finish around shoulder height. This should be about the same height that the swing was started from. When the sequence of the swing is out of the correct order (down, level, up) then the swing is generally too long. This long swing will not allow consistent contact. Many hitters will allow the bat to level off immediately. This will cause the sequence of the swing to be level, up and down at the finish with an early roll of the wrists.

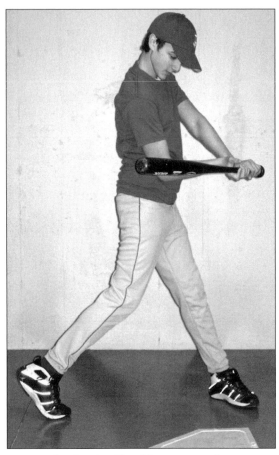

Bat levels off as hips are opening and lead arm straightens.

Good power position as back arm is continuing to extend. Palm up, palm down at contact.

◆ The tilt of the upper body at the hips will cause the lifting or uppercut action. This tilting action will be discussed at length later. It is important to realize, though, that even this slight upward action requires a compact swing. It is necessary to know the definition of the word compact as it will be used quite often from here on out. The dictionary definition of compact is "closely and firmly united" or "packed into a small space." These two definitions describe a good baseball swing. Keep in mind, though, that the follow through of a good swing is long through the hitting zone.

Head remains down with full extension until the wrists roll.

12. Contact
Most Common Problem – Rolling the wrists at contact
Coaching Tip – "Karate chop with the lead hand, punch with the back hand"

Once again we are at one of those mandatory positions that all good hitters arrive at in the sequence of a proper swing. The top hand has now shifted behind where the palm is now facing up. The bottom hand is now level with the top hand and the palm is facing down. The lead arm has straightened out to the ball and the back arm is in the process of straighten-

Power position at contact.

ing out also. Both arms will eventually be straight and extend as far as possible towards the pitcher until the wrists will eventually roll and the swing will continue to the middle of the upper back. The gradual leveling of the bat will usually allow the hands to get to the correct contact position and then be able to stay in the

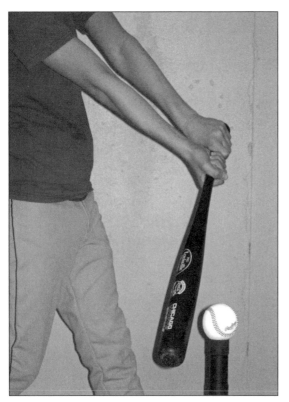

*Hips and hands squaring up to
the inside back of the ball.*

contact position for as long as possible. This is important so the bat can remain in the hitting zone for an extended period till the wrists will eventually roll. The good hitters will "whip" the bat with their finger, wrists and forearms without rolling the wrists at contact. This squaring of the bat at contact with the palm-up and palm-down approach is a fast action and not a static one because the bat doesn't slow up at all. The back arm may or may not be fully extended at contact depending on where contact is made in relation to the hitter's body. The hitter should continue on to full *extension* on all swings.

Many hitters will feel like they can get more bat speed by rolling the wrists at contact. The rolling of the wrists at contact is incorrect and this action will not allow good, consistent contact.

13. Hip Action
Most Common Problem – Lazy hip turn
Coaching Tip – "Drive the back knee to the pitcher"

If you will remember back, the first move of the hitter was the break of the back knee. This was the beginning of the hips opening toward the ball in a violent fast action. This is what is meant by opening the hips, and the hitter finishes with their belly button pointing at the pitcher. It is important to note that the *hips will open* in the same fast action *on every pitch*. The only exception is if the hitter is just slapping at the ball and not trying to drive it at all. Because the hands have to move away from the body slightly for the outer half pitch, the swing will be slightly less together on this pitch and thus the power is not as good on the outside pitch. The hips are just as fast, though.

14. Weight Shift
Most Common Problem – Keeping the weight on the back leg
Coaching Tip – "Throw your back side into the ball"

With the stride (#8) the weight is still on the back leg when the front foot lands. With the break of the back leg (first move #10, above) the weight will begin to shift towards the front side. This is accomplished by a violent turn of the hips towards the ball, with the front leg firming up and the head staying back or moving just slightly forward. This coordinated weight shift with the correct swing path will create the *bat speed and power* to the swing.

The hitter should maintain their balance throughout this action. They should feel like they are literally throwing the barrel into centerfield. This sends the hands on a linear path towards the ball as the hips rotate round. If the hitter throws the bat with all the explosive energy that they can muster the weight will shift into the ball.

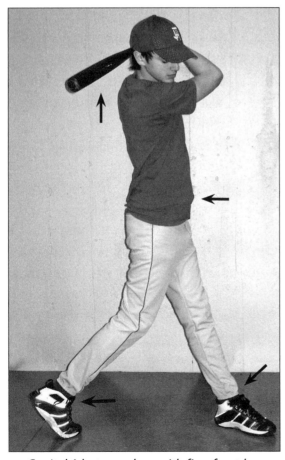

Capital A between legs with firm front leg.

Head down through contact.

Bat should be able to finish all the way to the middle of back.

15. Head, Eyes and Follow Through
Most Common Problem – Too much head movement and lack of lead arm extension.
Coaching Tip – "Steady head, see the ball and hit through it"

The hitter should keep the head steady throughout. This will allow the eyes to track the ball from the pitcher's hand to contact. The hitters should attempt to see the bat and ball meet. At completion of the swing the key points are:

a) The back heel is off the ground

b) The back instep, back knee and belly button are now facing the pitcher.

c) The chin is now on the back shoulder.

d) The area between the legs forms the letter capital "A" with a straight locked front leg.

e) Hands and bat will finish somewhere between the upper back and the top of the shoulders with two hands on the bat (not mandatory).

f) The front foot will probably have opened up slightly with the follow through. With the violent rotation of the hips this is almost unavoidable.

g) The hitter's head should finish on a line straight above the back hip with the upper body perpendicular to the ground. The ability to throw the bat and shift the weight as the head remains mostly back over this back hip is what makes a good hitter.

There is much debate over the aforementioned angle of the head and upper body at contact. For most hitters I believe this perpendicular position to be ideal with just a few exceptions. These fundamentals will be discussed further in the "Advanced Drills" and the "Other Hitting Topics" chapters.

▶ *Final Thought* ◀

One parental complaint I would receive from time to time is that I was teaching the hitters the "major league way" and their child was only a little leaguer. As a coach I felt it important to teach the fundamentals that the best players use. The object is still the same whether the player is facing major league pitching or little league pitching. Obviously, the expectations for the little leaguer will not be as high. Some concepts are too advanced for the young hitters but the fundamentals do not change. The coach should keep the terminology as simple as possible but teach the same fundamentals.

Drill Work

"Repetition, repetition and more repetition"

Hitters of all ages are continually striving to obtain the correct swing. There are very few natural swings. "Drill work" is necessary for working on obtaining the consistent swing in order to become a better hitter. One definition of the word drill is "to instruct by methodical exercises." A good hitting drill will instruct for itself. If a drill is done over and over, it can change or reinforce the muscle memory for the better.

1. A hitter gets timing from hitting a pitched ball; however, new habits and correct fundamentals are formed by doing good hitting drills.
2. It is very difficult to think and hit — so to be giving a ton of instruction on the fundamentals while a player is trying to hit a pitched ball can be counter productive. Save most of the instruction for the tee and flip drills.
3. A great drill will usually "force" the correct fundamental to be performed.
4. A good drill will help if performed correctly over and over again.
5. Usually, it is best to do a drill about 10 to 15 times in a row and then try to perform the same swing mechanic with the regular swing.
6. It is wise to have two bats for use. One should be a lighter, smaller bat and the other the hitter's regular bat. The lighter bat will be used for one hand drills and for increased repetition work.
7. There are many very good drills — try to perfect the basic ones before moving on to more advanced ones.
8. Many drills can be done alone with a ball on the tee or in a batting cage. However, some drills require another person to flip or pitch balls to the hitter.
9. Most hitters have natural tendencies, so it's important to find the drill or drills that most help that particular hitter.

10. Some drills are what I call "opposite drills" because they force the hitter to over exaggerate a certain action. This over-exaggeration, opposite of the hitter's normal actions, works as a counter balance correcting the hitter's form. Be careful of doing these drills too much as a new bad habit can occur. Generally, these opposite drills are very helpful even though people watching might be wondering what you are doing.

11. Some drills are multi-use drills. They work on more than one fundamental at a time.

► *Final Thought* ◄

Just to reiterate — the definition of a drill is to *instruct by methodical exercises*. Good drills instruct for themselves. The coach should provide the drills and a demonstration of how to perform them correctly. The coach should explain to the hitter why they are doing the particular drills. Good results will usually follow.

Five Drills To Teach The Fundamentals

The following 5 drills are a great start for learning the "perfect swing."

"Keeping it simple and producing greatness"

If you are doing these drills on a tee it is important to review the points made in the "step by step use of a batting tee" section. The coach and hitters should be especially mindful of points 11 and 12 in that section. Along the same line if the hitter is doing drills with a pitched ball, the goal is to always try to hit the ball in the direction of where it is pitched.

Drill # 1 – Pad Drill

Explanation – Have the hitter place a pad or fielder's glove under the armpit closest to the pitcher — the hitter will take a full swing and allow the pad to fall out after contact with the ball.

Goals of drill – This drill will help in a number of ways.

First, it will place the hitter in good hitting position (see Fundamental # 9). It is very difficult to be out of hitting position and hold the pad under the front arm.

Second, it will force the hitter to learn to use his forearms and hands in order to swing the bat.

Third, it will keep the front elbow and knob of the bat from lifting, and thus it won't allow the hitter to start the bat barrel on the wrong path to the ball.

Fourth, by allowing the pad to fall out on the follow through, it will force the hitter to get the proper extension with the hands and arms through the hitting zone.

◆ The hitting zone is the area out in front of home plate towards the pitcher where contact should be made.

◆ Be sure that the hitter still keeps his hands back towards the catcher with the pad so that he is in a strong and ready position. Also, make sure the hitter allows the pad to fall out on the follow through or he will develop an early roll of the wrists and thereby a lack of extension with the swing.

Pad establishes good hitting position and will force the hitter to use his hands.

Pad drops with correct extension.

Drill # 2 – Fake Flip Drill – Remember, once hitting position is established, it must be maintained. The fake flip drill is a good way of working on this.

Explanation – The coach is off to the side or directly in front (behind a screen) of the hitter. Holding a ball, the coach will go to flip the ball to the hitter. The coach has the option of holding on to the ball or of letting it go to the hitter.

Goals of Drill – As mentioned, the hitter needs to be able to take a controlled stride and maintain or go to proper hitting position. Hitters stride and prepare on every pitch but don't swing at every pitch. This drill will help in three ways.

First, this drill will make the hitter go to proper hitting position. If hitters come out of position when they stride, point it out and start over again.

Second, it will teach quickness and the compact swing mentioned above because the hitter will not be able to "cheat" and start early on the swing.

Third, confidence and understanding will start to develop in the hitter as he learns to wait for the ball to get to the hitting zone before starting the swing.

◆ Make sure the hitter takes the stride when the flip arm starts forward and doesn't stride and swing at the same time. Striding and swinging at the same time is a common mistake with some hitters.

> When taking regular batting practice it is sometimes a good idea to have the pitcher hold up on the pitch at the last possible moment in order to see how the hitter has reacted to this point. The good hitter will still be in a relaxed, confident mode just ready to begin the stride. The weaker hitter will probably already be moving in a way that is not conducive to good hitting position. This weaker hitter will usually begin to step out or will begin dropping the bat barrel too soon.

◆ The Drop Ball Drill #8 is also a good way to teach this action of maintaining good hitting position. Many hitters will begin to "cheat" while waiting for the coach to drop the ball. *Cheating* means to begin swinging way before the ball gets to the hitting area.

Drill # 3 – Fast Knee Drill – or Check Your Swing Drill

When a good hitter goes to swing but then holds up at the last second two things are seen. The hitter's back knee will fire towards the pitcher, and the hands of the hitter will start slightly forward with the knob of the bat still down. Remember, after the hitter has taken the stride and has maintained good hitting position (Drills 1 and 2 above), the first move of the hitter will come with an explosive break of the back knee and hip towards the ball.

The stride and swing are separate moves — stay back with stride.

Explanation – The hitter will take a stride and fire the back knee while holding up on the swing. The hitter's weight shifts forward but the hitter "checks" his swing. The knob of the bat remains down as the hands come forward a few inches.

Goals – First, the hitter must stay back in order to develop a fast back leg (if he lunges at all the back leg will not fire forward).

Second, the hitter will begin to develop a fast back knee and hips.

Third, the hitter will learn to keep the front elbow and knob of the bat down on the first movement, thereby keeping the barrel of the bat above the hands on the first move.

Fast back knee — knob down.

◆ The ideas of staying back and transferring the weight are very hard to teach, so this drill will help. It's good to have the hitter do this fast knee drill two or three times before swinging the bat each time. Do not let the hitter just turn his back foot fast. There should be a definite shift of weight where you see the hitter's weight move *from the back side towards the front foot*.

◆ When you observe a good hitter holding up on their swing at the last possible moment, this is known as "checking" the swing. You will notice the hitters' weight and hands have moved towards the ball but they don't swing.

Drill # 4 – Pull, Pivot, Push Drill

The hitter is in great hitting position from Drill # 1. The hitter is able to take his stride and maintain his proper ready position from Drill # 2 and they have an explosive back side from Drill # 3. We must now get the hitter to throw his hands at and through the ball.

Pull, Pivot, Push Drill.

Throwing hands to extension.

Explanation – Either using a much smaller bat or choking way up on their regular bat, the hitter will hold the bat only with the lead hand. With the top hand the hitter will straighten his fingers as if to make a karate chop and place it directly above the bottom hand touching the thumb of the lower hand. The hitter begins his swing with a slight pull with the lead hand towards the ball and then will proceed to straighten the lead arm as the top hand remaining on the bat will push the barrel through the ball. Remember, the top hand pushes the barrel through but does not grab on and hold the bat. The hitter will finish with the bat proceeding forward in only the lead arm. The top arm finishes pointing directly at the pitcher with the palm of the top hand pointing down and right at shoulder level. The hitter should also push with the back hip so that the hitter ends with the back heel up in the air and the chin up on the back shoulder.

Goals – First, the drill will give the hitter the feeling of throwing his hands at the ball without the front elbow rising up on the first move. Hitting with only the lead arm as in this drill, the knob will stay down getting the slight pull to begin the swing with the lead hand.

Second, this drill will give the hitter the feeling of pushing the top hand and the weight from the back side through as the lead arm extends.

Third, this drill will give the hitter extension from the arms while the head remains steady.

Fourth, this drill will give the hitter the understanding of what is meant by keeping his front shoulder in and not yanking it out away from the ball. (This will be discussed later.)

Fifth, having the chin end up on the back shoulder will teach the hitter how the head remains steady as the shoulders rotate.

◆ This drill should not be done with regular balls that are pitched at the hitter because the ball may strike the hitter's hands when swinging. Use softer balls or work on the tee with this drill.

◆ On most pitches, when we hit, it feels like we are throwing our hands way out towards center field. I like to have the hitter finish with his back hand only going as far as pointing towards center field because this will give him the understanding of keeping the front shoulder on the ball longer. With more experienced hitters you can begin to have them point the back hand in the direction of where the ball was pitched. It is important to have the hitter finish with the palm of the top hand facing down and only at shoulder level on completion of the swing in order to maintain a level swing. This may be a little complicated for younger hitters at first. They may have trouble keeping their top hand on the bat when they lead with the front arm. Over time, with practice, they will get the hang of it. Obviously, the hitter can hit with just the lead arm but this can put a lot of strain on the arm, and it does not always give the feeling of the proper direction and feel of throwing both hands and hip into the ball.

I've seen variations of this drill with different positions of the top hand, but I like the idea of the top hand pushing at the correct time and the resulting position of the top hand. This recommended hand position, though, can be dangerous if using hard balls in regular batting practice. Thus, the recommendation to use softer balls when doing this drill unless it is being done on a batting tee.

Drill # 5 – 1, 2, 3, 4 Drill – Finally, it is time to start to put all the pieces together. This drill will put the swing in "slow motion," so to speak.

Explanation – On the count of one, the hitter will take the stride going to 100 percent correct hitting position while landing on the ball of the front

1 – Stride and prepare to swing.   *2 – Back knee break.*

foot. On the count of two, the hitter will break the back knee slightly as the weight stays back but the front foot will go down. On the count of three the hitter swings as fast as possible with the proper weight shift. On the count of four the hitter freezes in the finish position with the hitter being able to see the bat come all the way around to the middle of the back with the chin finishing on the back shoulder and with two hands still on the bat (see # 14 above in the fundamental section).

Goals – First, the drill will make sure the hitter can perform and understand each move of the swing properly.

Second, the drill will make sure the hitter understands the correct sequence of moves with the proper swing (i.e., stride, back knee break, hands, barrel and extension).

Third, by having the hitter freeze on the finish we are ensuring a good balanced swing.

Fourth, by having the hitter keep two hands on the bat and being able to see the bat come around to the finish position, we ensure the correct hip rotation and that the head stays steady and down throughout the swing.

3 – Swing — steady head, eyes on ball.

◆ Remember, with regular hitting the front foot will actually land right before the ball reaches the hitting zone and not prematurely as in this drill.

◆ This is only a drill but necessary to teach the correct sequence of the swing. Many young hitters will not break the back knee before swinging. This leads to a lunging action which is not good.

◆ With actual game hitting the 1, 2, 3 and 4 actions will happen very fast. Also, for the purpose of the drill it is important to keep two hands on the bat all the way around. This will ensure the correct hip rotation. Many young hitters let go with the top hand before the finish because they lunge forward and do not turn properly, forcing them to let go with the top hand. The two hand finish versus the letting go of the top hand on the follow through will be discussed later.

4 – Finish under balance — bat around for correct hip turn.

▶ *Final Thought* ◀

A short explanation of hitting would be to stay back and explode with the hands and hips at the last second with the eyes on the ball the whole way. These five drills will help to develop those actions.

3 | Instant Feedback

"What you are doing and what you think you are doing are two different things"

"*Life is not always fair." "Keep working hard and things usually work out for the best." "Don't get too high and don't get too low — there is always tomorrow." These are some of the statements I remember my coaches telling our team over the years, usually when things were not going well. Obviously, they are a little heavy for the young players but there are many teaching moments that occur over the course of the season. And even though they were said in a baseball setting, they are obviously statements that can be used for any line of work. How the coach teaches the players to handle success and failure, winning and losing is one of the important roles of the coach and things that the players will use for other aspects of their lives.*

A common saying that we used to say back in the day was that the major leagues were "the easiest place to play but the hardest place to get to." This is very true to some extent — they have the best of everything — the best lights, fields, bats, pitchers with control, umpires, video of every at-bat, etc. Obviously, the difficult part was that the competition level was also the best. Getting to the big leagues is a whole other story. Only a very few that start out playing baseball as little leaguers ever reach the professional level. This doesn't mean that young players should not dream and try to reach that goal, but coaches and parents should keep it all in perspective and have the goal of getting their child to the high school level. From that point on it is pretty much out of the parent's hands and it will be up to the players as to how hard they want to work on the game.

Another of our sayings was that "if we had to play we may as well get some hits and win." Sometimes it is difficult for players to be motivated for whatever reason. It may be too cold or the other team may be much better. Remember to remind the players that conditions are generally the same for both sides and if you're going to play then you may as well give as close to 100 percent as possible. The coach and parent are responsible for teaching the players to only worry about what they can control — their effort level.

Finally, "losers make excuses" was another of the sayings that we were taught. Complaining and making excuses for losses or poor play never serves any purpose. The coach should teach young players to understand that errors and strike outs are part of the game and to learn from them and move on. We had a rule at our camps that the only players who could yell at a fellow camper were the players who had never made an error or never struck out before. That usually would quiet up the players and keep them accountable for their own play and not criticizing everybody else's play.

Many hitters can picture the correct swing and think they are doing it the correct way but in reality they are not. There must be a way of knowing if the swing and what the hitters are working on are correct. The hitters need to have some instant feedback when hitting to properly analyze the results of the swing. From my experience, a batting tee is still the best teaching aide for the proper analysis of the swing. One of my first questions to the parents or the hitter would be "do you have a useable batting tee?" The tee will allow the hitter a chance to groove the correct swing without having to worry about timing a pitched ball. It is important to see the flight of the ball off the tee so that you can analyze the height, direction and spin on the ball when it leaves the bat. As I have told the hitters I've worked with, "a three or four year old can hit a ball off a tee but that doesn't mean the swing is correct." Another common saying I've used is that "if you can't hit consistent line drives when a ball is sitting on a tee, how are you going to hit them when it is pitched to you?"

Unfortunately, many hitters believe that *batting tees* are only for the three to six year olds. By showing them the proper way of using the tee and of *analyzing their swing,* you can convince them of the importance of using this device. Remember, it is much more fun for a youngster to be hitting a ball than to be taking dry swings. All drills are safe to be done on a tee. If the parent and student are serious about improving, then the batting tee set up at home is a must. By the time a player reaches the high school level it is very important to have a tee setup at home so that they can get the proper amount of repetitions needed to stay sharp.

When a tee is not being used

If the hitter is just taking some dry practice swings without a ball, have them learn to swing at different pitch locations. Most hitters take their practice swing in the same location on every swing. Try to get the hitters to imagine pitches in different locations and then swing to those imaginary spots. Hitters with bad mechanical swings will have trouble getting the barrel to certain pitches (usually the knee-high pitch). Teach the hitters the nine different locations that the hitter can get a strike at, beginning with high and away, high down the middle and high and inside, etc. Have the hitters take dry swings trying to get the barrel to these different locations. This will be a good start towards the hitters learning to "visualize" also. This concept of visualization will be discussed later in the book. The hitter can place target balls on a backstop and work on swinging to these targets also.

If the hitter is working on his hitting with a pitched ball, how does the hitter know if the swing is correct or not? There are generally two things to look for:

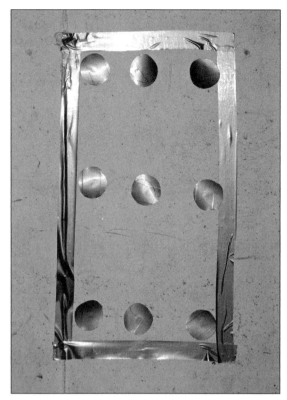

9 locations to practice the swing to.

1. Did the hitter hit the ball *solidly* — preferably a line drive? It is important to understand what is meant by the sweet spot on the bat. The sweet spot is the section of the bat between the trademark and the end of the bat. If contact is made in this spot the ball will travel off the bat the fastest. The hitter's goal is to hit every ball in this sweet spot area.

2. Did the hitter hit the ball in the *direction* of where the ball was pitched? Outside pitches should be hit to the opposite field, inside pitches should be pulled and pitches down the middle should be driven up the middle. Remember, the *location* of the pitch determines which direction the ball is hit and not the speed of the pitch. Assuming the hitter is getting good batting practice pitches, balls should be going to all fields, with a quarter of the hits going to left and right and the other half being hit between left center to right center fields.

Note: It is important to change speeds to the hitters occasionally during batting practice, even for the very young hitters. It is important that they understand the concept of timing and speed changes.

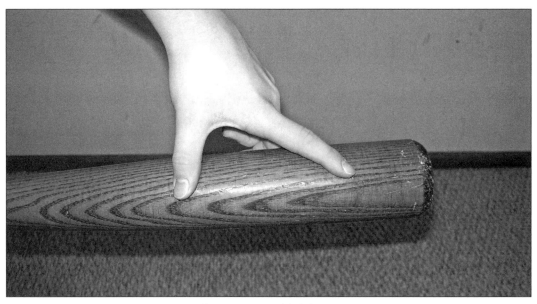

Sweet spot — hit it here.

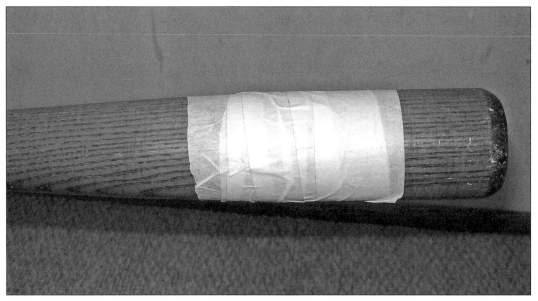

Tape on sweet spot will help you to know if the batters are hitting the ball in this area.

STEP BY STEP USE OF THE BATTING TEE

Note: The correct contact position is in front (towards the pitcher) of the hitter's body. This is the hitting zone as described earlier. The distance out front will vary depending on the location of the pitch, but unless you are working on a specific drill, the tee should be in front of the hitter.

Many coaches of young players set up the tee even with the hitter's belly button. This will make the point of contact way behind the correct position.

Caution: If a coach is putting the ball on the tee for the hitter, it is important to remind the hitter not to swing until you are totally out of the way.

1. Find a safe area where objects such as windows, televisions, people and pets are not in danger of being hit by the bat or ball. A little duct tape on the top portion of the stem of the tee will give it much longer life.

2. Find a reliable back stop like a net, an old sheet or blanket or a car tarp. A relatively inexpensive car tarp found at the hardware store already has the grommets in it and will be easy to hang in the basement or garage. Many hits off the tee may go straight up so you may need to put some protection above the tee area also.

3. Any kind of ball should work — use something safe. Tennis balls and rag balls are fine, if using a hard ball is unsafe. A whiffle ball tends to be too light to feel how well the ball is being hit though but it is very safe.

Tee and net set up.

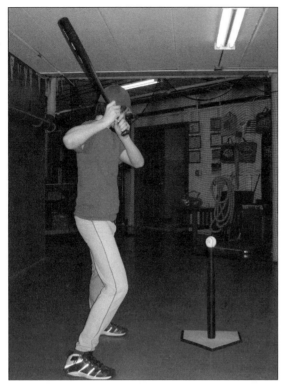

The further the distance from the net the better (if possible) — this will allow the hitter to see the ball's flight.

Setting up a home plate first and then setting a tee down is ideal.

4. Be sure to find a good solid tee that will last more than a few hits. Don't forget the duct tape in a few key spots to avoid premature wear and tear. There are some advanced tees out on the market that are very good but not necessary if you follow these guidelines.

5. The further away from the backstop that you can set the tee and hitter the better. Many balls appear to be hard hit from a short distance but once again, the flight of the ball off the tee is important in order to properly analyze the swing. If there is not room to back up very far, then put some *targets* up on your backstop that will indicate direction and height of the hit ball.

6. The hitter must treat the base of the tee as if it is a regular home plate and line up the same distance away from the plate as they do in the game. Many hitters will feel like they are too close to the tee when they do this, but you must explain to them that it is paramount to stand the same distance away as in a game in order to get the correct swing and results. Ideally, put down a regular home plate first and have the hitter line up with that, then place your tee down.

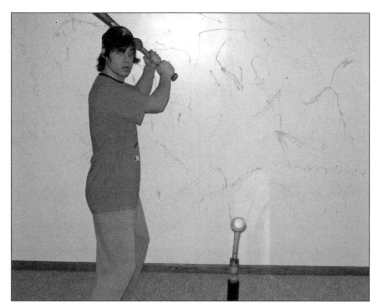

Eyes start at pitcher with tee work. Hitters track ball in their minds, prepare, stride and swing with head and eyes dropping to the ball.

7. It is important to have the hitter begin with *his eyes out toward the pitcher to start*, before each swing, as if he is tracking the ball from the pitcher to contact. Try not to let the hitter stare at the ball and keep his eyes glued on the ball before hitting it. Another great way of doing this is to flip a ball out in front of the hitter and have him wait until the ball hits the ground before swinging. This will give him the idea of tracking and waiting for the ball and obviously not just staring at it on the tee.

8. Because contact should be made out front (towards the pitcher), and because most tee stems are in the middle of the plate, the hitter needs to move back towards the catcher. (The hitter should move a half foot back for a low pitch and 1 foot back for a high pitch.)

9. The swing goal is to hit line drives the *same height* as the height of the tee. Remember, this is one of the indicators telling us whether the swing is correct or not.

10. In order to hit consistent line drives the hitter should hit the top portion of the tee and the back portion of the ball to create good back spin on the ball. If they are hitting all ball and no tee, then they are topping the ball, resulting in hitting only ground balls. Many times even with a good line-drive-inducing swing, the tee will keep falling over. Simply add some weight to the tee's base so the tee doesn't have to be picked up continually. Obviously, if the hitter is swinging under the ball the results will be missed balls or pop ups.

Low pitch set up down middle hit back through middle for good fundamental swing.

High tee for compact swing and staying on top.

11. **Drill # 6 – Knee High Pitch through Middle**

The hitter should work on the *low pitch* (knee high) *for the mechanics* of the swing. If the hitter is set up properly (see numbers 4 & 5), the pitch is located right down the middle, and a correct swing will be to hit the ball directly up the middle. In other words, a knee-high line drive up the middle would be the ideal hit on this pitch. Until the hitter can take 8 or 9 out of 10 hits right back through the middle, don't be satisfied that they have the right swing. A hitter's hands and hips will have to square up correctly in order to hit the ball consistently back through the middle with authority. Most hitters do not like to put the ball that low on the tee, but it is necessary to get the fundamentals of the swing down.

12. **Drill # 7 – High Tee**

The hitter should work on the *high pitch* (chest high or a little above) *for a shorter, more compact swing.* Concentrate on staying on "top" of the ball and not popping it up. The hitter should not worry so much about trying to hit this pitch back through the middle as should be done on the knee high pitch.

Once again, the correct hit on this pitch is a line drive the same height as the top of the tee. Putting the tee on a chair may be necessary to work on this pitch for tall hitters. Remember a protective net for above the tee also.

Once again, with the high pitch make sure the tee is further out front towards the pitcher before working on this pitch. The reason is that it takes our arms longer to extend on the high pitch. Thus, the hitter needs to be quicker and stronger in order to hit the ball out front and to have a chance to not pop it up or swing and miss on this pitch.

13. After working on the low pitch for the fundamentals of the swing and the high pitch for a more compact swing, the hitter should proceed to inside and outside pitches. Remember, the hitter must remain standing the correct distance away from home plate as in a game and adjust the tee accordingly.

For the outside pitch, set the tee on the outer (further from hitter) portion of home and just slightly out front of the front knee, approximately one inch. For the inside pitch, place the tee on the inside (closer to the hitter) portion of home plate and out front more, approximately a foot and a half.

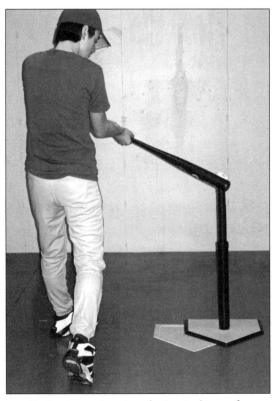

Notice tee set up in relation to home for outside pitch. Drive ball to opposite field.

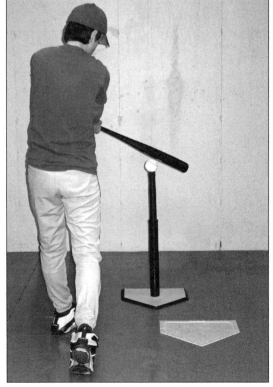

Notice tee set up for inside pitch — drive ball to pull side of field.

This helps the hitter understand the different points of contact on different pitch locations. If the hitter can consistently hit the knee-high pitch through the middle (Drill # 6) and stay on top of the ball on the high tee (Drill # 7), the inside and outside pitches should come along pretty easily. However, it is important to understand that pitches on the corners of home plate are tougher to hit in games than pitches down the middle.

The inside and outside tee drills are best done in a full batting cage. Otherwise, the hitters must be cautious of their surroundings. It may be necessary to angle the hitter and the tee if only a front net is used.

14. **Drill # 8 – Dropped Balls**

This is a drill for times when a tee is not available or after some good tee work. Obviously, a parent or coach is needed for the dropped ball drill. I've found it to be much more challenging and productive than the side soft toss flips. The problem with the popular side toss flip drill is that the ball will have a slight arc on it. This will allow the hitter to get away with a long or uppercut swing.

Explanation of Dropped Ball Drill: An adult stands to the side and slightly out front of the hitter. After the player strides the ball is dropped either immediately or after a short delay. The player will have to be very quick on the dropped ball. Any wasted motion will make them late and they will miss the ball. This is a great way to develop a quicker, more compact swing and to challenge the hitter. Young players may get a little frustrated at first but have them hang in there and they will improve.

It is important that the coach drops the ball and does not flip it. They should pull their hand up and away after dropping the ball. This dropped ball drill can be used for many of the drills in this book also.

Caution: The coach should not lower the hand into the swing path after letting go of the ball. Either keep the hand there or pull it up and away.

The dropped ball will require great hand-eye coordination and a quick swing.

15. For the serious player who has neither a tee nor a person to do the dropped ball drill, refer to the advanced Drill # 45 in the "Advanced Drills" chapter of this book. This will at least give the player an opportunity to take some swings at a ball and not just hit air.

16. Finally, the use of a mirror can be helpful when just taking some dry swings and working on hitting position, etc.

▶ *Final Thought* ◀

Coaches, remember to encourage each player to have a workable batting tee set up at home. There will be a greater likelihood of them practicing and improving on their hitting if they have a tee. Make sure the players know how to set up on it properly with the correct distance away from home as discussed. Otherwise, it may not help. Drills # 6 and 7 are very important and can be used for checking for correct swings while using any other drill. Hitting the ball solidly is always the first goal. The second goal would be to hit the ball in the direction of where it was pitched. Remember, it is better to take 20 fundamentally correct swings than to take 100 random swings that are not fundamentally correct.

4 | Having Fun

"How can it be fun when I never get a hit?"

The year 1984 was a good year for me. Looking back after the season, though, I often wondered if it was any fun. The intensity level that I had to maintain was very grueling and something I could not duplicate again in my career. Obviously, I played with and against a lot of great players. The two I was most in awe of were George Brett and Eddie Murray. The great ones like these two seem to be able to play with a relaxed intensity that I could not imitate. If I went out and said I was going to relax and have fun, I never seemed to play well. On the other hand when I would go out with all the intensity I could muster, the results were good, but when I looked back it wasn't that much fun. Trying to balance the intensity level along with having fun is one of the goals and challenges of every athlete. Most players won't know what it is like to be a star at the major league level, but everyone can learn to compete with intensity and to have fun.

Coaches and parents can definitely help with this goal. Leaving the games for playing and using the practices for coaching is one of the keys to having focused players. It is very difficult to perform well in a game if the mind is on different mechanical things. Trying to hit with any or even a few swing thoughts is very difficult. Keeping the players focused on the ball is the best advice in the game.

Keeping a player's mind focused and in the moment is crucial to success. Worrying about what the coach or parent is going to think when the game is over is not fun. Coaches and parents need to try to balance the amount of intensity and "just have fun" attitudes, too. There is nothing wrong with expecting an intense focus from the players as long as it is balanced with having fun also. Obviously, this is easier said than done but so important to the players' development to be as good as they can be.

One of the most used and overused sayings in sports is "just go out and have fun." I say overused because so often the saying is used after the coach or parent has made it close to impossible for the kids to have fun. What appears to be fun for the parents isn't always fun for the participants. Sitting on the bench, striking out, standing around in the outfield, listening to a long speech, listening to a parent screaming from the sidelines, having a coach "show up" or ridicule a player (any player) is not fun to a youngster. These are just some examples and I'm sure you can think of more but you get the idea. Fun is *feeling good about oneself.* It is not that simple to just go out and have fun, especially with such a difficult game.

Winning is generally more fun than losing so I believe it is OK to play to win. However, the emphasis should be on developing players and having fun. If the coach concentrates on these two objectives, then they will be surprised by how often the winning follows. After all, there are two signs of a good coach. First, is the team better at the end of the season than at the beginning of the season? Second, does each of the players want to keep playing the following season? If coaches can say yes to these then they have done a great job.

It is important to understand what fun is for the young players so that we can recognize why they may not be having it. Why do many kids nowadays prefer to play video game baseball more than the real thing? Is it because when kids play video games they have a chance to compete and succeed? Is it because it keeps their minds occupied and the games are constantly changing and challenging them? Is it because they continually get a little better at the game each time they play the video game? Is it because there is not an "expert" next to them constantly yelling out instructions to the player? Is it because they create a bond with the other players they may be playing with? I think yes to all of these questions.

With this in mind I will try to define what having fun is to the young player. I've conducted hundreds of camps and clinics over the years and have had the opportunity to observe what most kids enjoy doing.

1. Just having a chance to compete is fun
2. Staying busy
3. Variety
4. Being challenged
5. The feel of success
6. Games and contests
7. A caring coach
8. A smile and a high five

Let's explore these a little more in depth.

1. **A chance to compete** – As mentioned above, sitting on a bench is not generally fun. It may be for a short time but most kids want the opportunity to compete and feel a part of the team. It is the responsibility of the coach to keep each player involved and to make each player feel a part of the team no matter how little they contribute. A lasting bond is formed among teammates that feel like they are contributing to a common goal.

   Using your practice time in a productive manner is essential for this goal. It is a great time to give each player an equal chance to compete as they are bonding with teammates. One example of this would be moving your players around to different positions at practice. Allowing them the opportunity to play the position they like to play, and not just the position they play in a game, is important and fun. Mixing up the lineup during practice games is another way of giving confidence to the weaker hitters. Good coaches will think of other ways to include everyone, remembering that all deserve an equal chance to compete.

2. **Staying Busy** – Baseball has enough slow time built in to it already so try to keep the kids moving and working on their game as much as possible. With help from other coaches or parents set up different stations where the players are doing a lot. Practice time will fly by and the kids won't dread practice. Keep the long talks and the warm up time to a minimum. It generally does not take long for young players to get loose and too much time may lead to boredom or worse — "messing around."

3. **Variety** – Nobody likes doing the same thing over and over. Mix up the practice agenda as often as possible. Giving players the opportunity to play different positions will make each player excited and feel more important. Using different hitting, pitching and fielding drills are a good idea, too. The coach needs to do some homework so he can provide variety in these areas.

4. **Being Challenged** – Like playing the video games, most kids like to be challenged. It's up to the coach to treat each player separately and challenge them to their ability level. When something becomes easy the monotony and boredom will start to set in and that is when many young players will not want to play anymore. Let the players know that you will be challenging

them differently so they don't think you are picking on them. Challenging the player up to the point where frustration is about to set in and then backing off is important.

5. **The Feel of Success** – Video games are fun because the players tend to get a little better each time they play. Advancing to a new level spurs them on to want to play again and again till they beat the game. They usually get the feeling that they are accomplishing a little more each time and feel successful. The more success they have the more determination they have to play again and win.

It is this feeling of success that we want to incorporate into their minds when playing baseball. This is a tricky one because obviously there are ups and downs in sports. One never can totally beat the game. Baseball can be especially difficult because even though the players are part of a team, it is very much an individual challenge of player versus the ball. Furthermore, all the action is out in the wide open for all to see, thus making it a high pressure game. Therefore, it is important for the coach to teach patience to the players and more important to look for little indicators that the player is improving. *Pointing this improvement out to the player and to the player's parent* is very important. If players feel like they are advancing a little

Smiling faces — a coach's dream.

at a time they will want to keep playing and working on it. The more they feel like success is right at their fingertips the more determined they will become. The feel of success will breed *determination* and the good coach can foster these feelings of success. The thought of having a whole team of determined and *motivated players* is a coach's dream and is attainable with the proper coaching and motivation.

The opposite end of this is when the player stops feeling successful and the determination seems to stop. Sometimes there is nothing a coach can do in this instance. In my opinion most kids stop playing a particular sport when they stop having the feeling of improving at it and not because of burnout as we often think. Without this "feel" of some success it is difficult to want to keep playing that particular sport.

6. **Games and Contests** – Kids generally love to play games and to have contests where they have a chance to win. I say generally because they don't necessarily enjoy games where the pressure to win and to do great are involved. Parents and coaches who put too much emphasis on winning and performing great are not helping kids to enjoy the games. Little contests where each player has a chance to win are fun. Having little hitting, throwing, fielding or pitching contests is usually fun as long as there are different winners from time to time. The coach should handicap the contests in some way so each player will have an equal chance. However you handicap the contest, let the players know why you are doing it and they will understand. Playing regular baseball games are fun for players. A few innings to finish practice is usually a lot of fun and a nice reward for their hard work earlier at practice.

7. **Caring Coach** – Notice I didn't say a knowledgeable coach. This would be a nice bonus but it is not mandatory for kids to have fun. Caring is obviously the most important ingredient here. A coach who puts each player's needs first and genuinely cares that the players improve is the key to *kids' development*. If the coach is positive and enthusiastic along with being caring and knowledgeable, then you are lucky and have a great coach. It is not always possible to have a volunteer coach who has all these qualities, but once again caring is the key. As I mentioned earlier in this book, I've seen players improve tremendously without much instruction just by being challenged by a coach who cares.

The key to putting the player's interests first is communication. It's important that the coach attempts to get to know each player as much as possible. Questions about favorite players, other sports they like to play and other interests are a good way to start getting to know the players. Letting the players know that you care for them beyond what they can do for you on the playing field is important.

A coach who tends to ridicule any player on the team will adversely affect every player on the team. Let me repeat this thought: the ridicule will affect everyone on the team. So coaches should be careful of this habit even if it is directed at their own son or daughter.

8. **Smile and High Five** – The coach or parent who can recognize a good effort by the players and tell them this at the end of the day is crucial to having each player want to come back and do it again the next practice, game or season.

So let's put the above points into the context of teaching young hitters to have fun while working on their swings.

Give the Hitter a Chance – Remember, it is one thing to have a chance but another thing to have a chance to compete. This means that the player is not totally overmatched and has a chance of getting a hit. It is no fun for the player to have no confidence and feel like they really don't have a chance to succeed. The responsibility also lies with the parents to try to put their children at the proper level of play so that they are not totally overwhelmed. Some ways of giving the hitters a better chance are:

a) Set up a nice working hitting area at home where the hitter can either work alone or with help from a parent. Refer to the Instant Feedback section, Chapter 3, for help with getting set up. After a rough game, a few swings on a tee can give the hitter hope for the next game.

b) A good, concise explanation of the things that you want the hitters to work on at the beginning of practice is important. Be sure to emphasize the "why" of the drills or program. The young hitters may not fully understand why you are having them work on a specific area but in time they will.

c) If there are specific problem areas refer to the chapter on "Problem Solving" and work on the suggested drills.

d) If the young player is interested, taking some private or group lessons is a good option for building confidence and giving her a better understanding of what needs to be done to improve.

Staying Busy – For the team, remember to get help from other coaches or a parent or two. Set up different hitting stations. At each station, the hitters should be working on different hitting drills. A good explanation of why they are doing each drill should be given. The coaches should stay *attentive to detail* so that the players perform the drills correctly. This may mean teaching your helpers to know what to look for.

Giving a long talk about hitting usually will bore the players. Giving short talks on different aspects of hitting with some demonstration is usually much more productive.

Give individual players a little routine of drills to perform at home and if the parent can be with them that would be great. Playing some of the child's favorite music while hitting is good for developing rhythm and breaking up any monotony that may occur.

Variety – Working on different drills is important. If the drill is done correctly, the results will show when the hitter goes back to their regular action. Then the coach and players should move on to another drill. When the hitters begin to get bored with tee work move on to the dropped ball drills or soft toss work. Going out to the local batting cages or to the field for regular batting practice is always a good idea but drill work should not be forgotten. Continual reinforcement of some good drills is how the swing can improve the most. Remember, live hitting will help timing but not usually change the mechanics of the swing.

Being Challenged – This is a must for improvement and avoiding boredom. Athletes in general are competitive and will generally raise their level of play to meet the challenge. Challenging weaker players is important so that in time they will be able to compete at the level they are playing at. It is just as important to challenge the very good player so they don't get bored because things are too easy.

Finally, challenges are equally necessary for the successful player who has relied on his athleticism to be successful but who has some flaws in his mechanics. Challenging this type of player will sometimes make him realize that he needs to improve his mechanics for the future, even though he has been successful up till now. It is very difficult to convince this type of player that the methods that they are doing now will not work in the future. In a positive way let the player's parents know how you are trying to help the player improve.

Don't assume that challenging a hitter always means throwing faster to them. Just as important is learning to adjust to slower pitching and learning to hit curve balls. I never thought a hitter was too young to teach how to hit the curve ball, even one as young as seven years old. I was always using a soft rag ball at the time, though, just in case it didn't break.

The Feel of Success – Notice I said it's important that players feel like they are successful. It may not be noticeable in their statistics yet, but it is important that they think they are improving so their hard work is paying off. As coaches we certainly don't want to give false praise to the hitters, but it is important to have the hitters believe that they are progressing. This can be tough if the hitter doesn't see the results in the form of hits. It's very important that the parents and coaches keep emphasizing improvement and not hits. Over time this will pay off as the players improve and the kids don't get down on themselves. Remember coaches, stay positive and watch for little signs of improvement and be sure to point this out to each and every player.

Games and Contests – You can keep the hitters much more engaged by making a little contest or game of their batting practice. Whether they are working on drills or regular batting practice you can have the hitters competing against each other or against their previous best result or even against the coach if desired. Assign a point value to certain hits and pit team against team or player against player. Remember to handicap the contest if needed so each player or team has an equal chance of winning. Divide the sides up equally or pitch differently to the players depending on their ability levels. There are many ways of doing this. Picking sides among the team and competing as little groups is fun as long as the teams are somewhat equal. A few examples of group or individual contests are:

a) Set up a target the hitters try to hit or a certain field that they must hit the ball into.

b) Assign point values to hard hit balls — 1 point for hard hit ground balls, 3 points for line drives and 5 points for long drives.

c) The player gets to keep hitting as long as they keep putting the ball in play or the defense doesn't get them out.

d) Put the hitters in game-like situations. Have bunting, hit and run, game winning hit and sacrifice fly contests.

e) Give the hitters different counts that they will encounter and see how they respond — 3 and 2 counts with 2 outs and the bases loaded is a famous one. It's important to put the hitters into these type of pressure situations in practice because it can help them if that situation occurs in a real game.

These are just some examples. All kids will enjoy participating in hitting contests. Keeping it fair where each player has a chance to win is the key to maintaining good effort and keeping it fun for the players. You can definitely stretch the amount of time that a player is willing to keep working on their hitting by having contests. This is good to do even with hitting drills. Using simple rewards like baseball cards can be a useful and a fun thing also. I never liked to use rewards all the time, though, because the players would play more for the rewards than for the idea of improving.

A Caring Coach – Obviously the player will know that their own parent will care how they perform, but sometimes this is the problem. Parents can care too much. This puts a lot of undue pressure on their child. If hitting sessions always end up with someone upset, the parent may want to look for another hitting coach for their son or daughter. The other alternative is to continue to work with their son or daughter, but the parent should hold the advice to a minimum. Have your child perform different drills without much instruction. Be sure to try the tips given in the "Be the Coach You Were Meant to Be" chapter.

Keeping it short and to the point.

For the coach of a team here are some ways to show you care.

    a)   Work with each player an equal amount of time.

    b)   Show equal enthusiasm and equal patience with each player.

    c)   Mention something positive to each player's parents when possible.

    d)   Give individual or team homework also when possible.

    e)   Always point out any little improvements that you notice.

Acknowledging a Job Well Done – A good "wrap up" is as important as a good opening to the session. Explain the things that were worked on during the practice and the reason for those things. Tell the players how proud of their effort you are and how much their hard work will pay off eventually, if not sooner. All should feel good about their practice time and hopefully look forward to the next time together.

▶ *Final Thought* ◀

Each player has a different personality and it's important for the coach to watch for indications that a player may be unhappy. The two most telling signs that a player is not having fun are: the player who seems totally bored or the player who doesn't get along with his teammates. Remember, showing the unhappy player that you care can make all the difference for that player's mindset in the immediate and long term future. Talking to this player more and making him feel important to the team can help. Letting the unhappy player be captain for the day and giving them a little extra attention almost always helps.

5 | **Advanced Hitting Drills**

"Baseball is a game of repetition — challenges and variety erase boredom"

A frequent question I would be asked by students (besides, What teams did you play for) was, "How many home runs did you hit?" I liked to tell them in a round about way. Once at a banquet with the great Ernie Banks, I was sure to mention that Ernie and I had combined for 514 big league home runs, hoping that the audience didn't realize that Ernie had 512 of those. Obviously, power was not my forte. I try to tell the students that home runs are the reward for doing everything right. They are not something to try for but will happen if the hitter performs the fundamentals of hitting correctly. Every athlete has different size, with some naturally bigger and stronger. For young players, I define power with this question: "Can you hit a solid ground ball that can get through the infield?" If the hitter can consistently do that then they have power.

For the small or weaker player don't panic. Obtain and stay with a good fundamental swing and sooner or later they will grow and get stronger. The hitter can work on gaining strength also. Most high school programs will encourage and coordinate a weight lifting program. Before that age the hitter can do basic strengthening exercises, with the most important being exercises that build up the hands, wrists and forearms. The most funda-mentally sound players and not the strongest are the ones who advance.

After practicing the fundamental Drills # 1 through #8, the hitters should begin to work on some of the advanced drills in this chapter. Remember, a drill should isolate a certain area of the swing so that done correctly, the muscle memory taught overcomes the bad muscle memory. When I say advanced drill, it doesn't necessarily mean it is harder to perform, but it might mean that you need two people or some special apparatus to perform the drill. Remember, earlier in this book I described some drills as opposite drills. These drills aren't necessarily fundamentally correct but are designed to go to the opposite extreme. The correct motion is between the extremes of the opposite drills and the hitter's normal, but incorrect actions.

Most hitters have natural tendencies in their swing. Some of these tendencies are good and some are bad. The bad tendencies are so natural that if they get away from certain drills, then those tendencies will reappear and the bad habits will begin to creep back into the swing. Identify what those negative tendencies are to isolate the particular drills that help this area. Once these drills are identified the hitter should never go too long without doing these particular drills that overcome his natural bad tendencies. Over an extended period of time these bad habits may altogether disappear, which is the ultimate goal.

The advanced drills which cover the fundamentals at which the hitter is strong at may not be needed but it is good to review them occasionally. The variety of drills that the hitter performs can prevent boredom from setting in. I was continually telling the hitters that the drills they found the hardest to perform and perfect were the drills they should be doing the most. This is not always fun but usually necessary.

I have put these drills into categories and in the order of the fundamentals that were covered in "The Fundamentals" chapter. Following each fundamental are some drills that reinforce that fundamental. These drills will help to form the correct muscle memory for a great swing.

You will notice that some drills are multi-use drills that can be used to develop more than one habit.

Fundamental 1 – Bat Size

I was never big on the holding-out-the-bat-for-so-many-seconds drill. Using the bat chart in Chapter 1 should be a good guide. You should be able to tell the correct bat size by looking at the size of the bat compared to the size of the hitter and recognize if it seems too long or too short. Remember, an ounce either way shouldn't matter, but the length is important. One indicator that may help is the distance the hitter gets away from home plate. If they get very close the bat may be too short, and if they get too far then the bat may be too long. Along the same lines if the hitter seems to get jammed a lot when hitting then maybe they should try a little shorter bat. On the other hand if many balls are hit on the end of the bat then maybe a little longer bat may help. Usually there are other reasons for why they are not hitting the ball on the "sweet spot" of the bat, but changing the bat size may be a way of starting to eliminate possible problem areas. If a bat seems too long, the hitter can choke up on it to shorten the length. A 32 inch bat becomes a 31 inch bat by choking up an inch.

Correct grip and grip pressure are necessary for good contact and speed.

Fundamental 2 – Grip

The method used in Chapter 1 is good so the bat gets into the upper palm just at the beginning of the finger line. But to get the proper *pressure in the hands and forearms* is tough, especially for young kids. Many hitters tend to squeeze the bat too tight and restrict the quickness and bat speed in the swing. Ideally, when waiting for the pitch the grip should be very light with the bat almost being able to fall out of the bottom hand and just slightly firmer with the top hand. As the pitch is approaching and the hitter prepares the bat, the grip should automatically firm up, especially in the top hand so that that barrel doesn't get "left behind." Keeping tension out of the hands and arms is a good thing and will lead to quickness. A tension-free start is easier said than done for nervous or over-anxious hitters. It is possible to have too loose a grip also to the point where the hitter can't control the bat barrel through the swing. Putting the bat too far up in the fingers can cause this lack of control.

On a scale of 1 to 10, with 10 being the tightest grip, the hitter should start with a 3 or 4 while waiting for the pitcher to start their delivery. Keeping a light grip right before swinging will keep the tension out and allow hitters to be quick with their hands. Right when they are ready to swing the grip pressure moves up to about a 7, making sure to feel the bat barrel.

Fundamental 3 – Plate Position

The most common position to set up in the batter's box would be with the front foot even with the corner where the plate breaks back towards the tip. Obviously, hitters have their own preferences about whether to be up front in the box or way in the

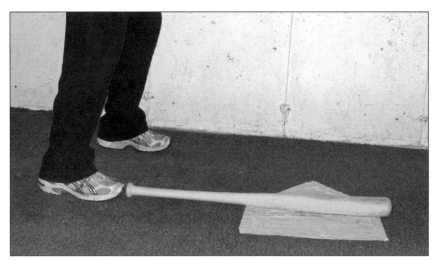

For young hitters to understand correct distance from home.

back. But being at the corner may help with stride length because it is 8 inches from this corner to the front of home plate.

Method 1 – For very young hitters you can actually have them put the bat down so that the end of their bat is one inch beyond the outside corner. The young hitter will then put the toes of his lead foot against the knob end of his bat and then separate his feet into a balanced position as he picks up his bat.

Method 2 – For the more experienced hitter using the method in "The Fundamentals" chapter under plate positioning should suffice. The use of a balance beam as talked about next is also a great method to keep the feet aligned.

Fundamental 4 – Feet Alignment
Drill # 9 – Balance Beam – Stance and Feet Alignment
An excellent device for feet alignment and balance is a balance beam. This can be made very easily (even I did it) by getting two 4-by-4-inch pieces of wood about 5 feet long. Cut the one piece in half and attach one 2-and-½-inch piece to each end with a couple of door hinges. Building a balance beam is one of the best things you can do for the serious hitter. The beam can be used in a number of ways to teach correct feet alignment.

   1.   The beam placed in front of the hitter towards home plate can be used to establish their distance from home, a good even alignment of their stance and the direction of the hitters' stride foot.

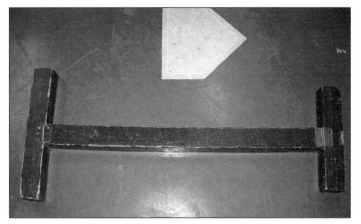

Balance Beam — great teaching tool.

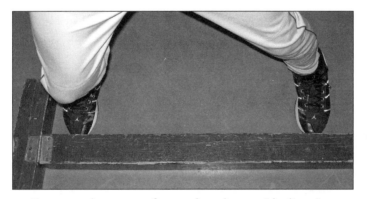

Beam used to square feet and work on stride direction.

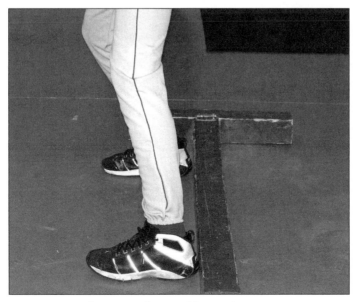

Beam used to avoid stepping out.

Beam used to avoid over-striding.

Balls of feet and balance development.

2. The beam can be set behind the hitter's feet to help the hitter from bailing out with the front foot or from sliding the back foot around when swinging.

3. The beam can obviously be used to work on the stride length also. Setting one end of the beam a few inches in front (towards the pitcher) can prevent a long stride.

4. Finally, and most important, having the hitter stand on top of the beam will develop balance throughout the swing. This balance development may take time but is essential for becoming a good hitter.

Caution: Regular batting practice should not be taken with the hitter on a balance beam. Their ability to get out of the way of a pitch thrown at them is limited. Tee work or short flip work is recommended.

Fundamental 5 – Balance
Drill # 10 – Swing Balance

Standing on the balance beam while swinging is a great tool for developing balance throughout the swing. For many, just standing on it will be difficult at first, but this is a great way to teach hitters how to be on the balls of their feet and to start with balance. Hitters should swing their normal swing with regular stride and full bat speed, remaining on the beam to a complete finish of their swing. Once again, this drill easily shows any loss of balance. Hitters who continually fall forward towards home plate when swinging are usually collapsing their back hip and shoulder. Hitters who continually fall back away from home are usually pulling their front shoulder and have an improper weight shift.

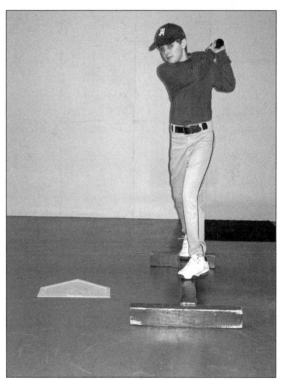

Balance, Jimmy.

- Remember, the hitter should swing at game speed. Start with trying to get one fully balanced swing and then try to improve on the consistency.
- You may have to put a weighted object at the back corner of the beam to keep it from sliding if on a very smooth surface and for larger hitters.

Fundamental 6 – Upper Body and Bat Starting Position

It is at this stage that actions are critical for producing a good fundamental hitter. The fake flip or even fake pitch drills explained previously are very important when trying to teach the proper hitting position when the hitter strides. Don't forget the pad drill explained in Chapter 1 for maintaining a good bat angle when preparing to swing.

Drill # 11 – Holding Bat with One Arm – Alternate Hands

The hitter should hold her regular bat with one hand only. Younger players may have to choke up some and this is OK. The hitter will take some strides with just one hand on the bat. The hitter should alternate each hand on the bat to get the correct position with each individually. With one hand holding the bat, the hitter should keep the bat in the fundamentally correct position because to do otherwise will make the bat very heavy and hard to maintain in the correct position. If the hitter allows the knob of the bat to point anywhere but down the bat barrel will become very heavy and tough to hold for long.

Top hand for correct alignment —
trademark above back shoulder.

Lead arm for bat alignment — light
and ready in this position.

Drill # 12 – Weighted Bat

The hitter puts a heavy weight like a bat donut on the barrel end of the bat. Have the hitter take some strides preparing to swing. With the heavy weight on the end, the hitter will feel the barrel if it begins to fall because of the weight of the barrel. In slow motion, have the hitter guide the weighted bat through the strike zone slowly.

Weighted barrel to feel bat barrel position. Arms can stay relaxed with this bat angle.

◆ We are not swinging with these drills, just taking the stride and preparing to swing in order to get the feel of where the bat head is at all times. The problem with hitting with aluminum bats is that they tend to feel so light that the hitters never can feel the barrel of the bat and thus don't realize that it is coming out of hitting position or that it is not on the proper path to the ball.

◆ A great teaching tool is the use of video analysis or digital computer analysis. If these tools are available then use it occasionally to let the hitter see the position of the bat as the front foot lands. As they say, "seeing is believing," and this will convince the hitter that the bat may not be getting to the right hitting position. A more easily available tool is a *mirror,* which will help the students to observe what they are doing with the bat barrel. Watching their actions in front of the mirror will help them understand where the barrel is at this stage of the swing sequence.

Fundamental 7 – Trigger (Preparation) – Drills

A couple of points are worth repeating. Prepared hitters are better than unprepared hitters. Things in motion tend to be quicker and more prepared than static things. The great hitters prepare. If the hitter is naturally very static but fundamentally sound then it may not be mandatory at the lower levels of baseball as long as her weight starts on the back foot. Make sure the hitter is as fundamentally sound as possible before teaching her a trigger action. Remember, if she has to think about

Hands start forward.

Will load by moving the hands back.

To ready position. One way of triggering the bat to ready position.

getting the bat ready, or the trigger makes her come out of good hitting position, then the development of this preparation action may not be worth it. With older, more experienced hitters it will be easier to develop a trigger action, but it still takes time. They must get through the "thinking about it stage" before it becomes a natural action. Remember, the key is making sure the hitter gets the weight over the back leg before striding and being ready to swing. A trigger is usually good because *things in motion are quicker than things that are still.* They tend to keep tension out of the body also.

Here are three trigger drills to try.

Drill # 13 – Front Shoulder Load

The hitter starts in the perfect hitting position as described in the fundamental chapter. Have the hitter close the front shoulder back slightly towards the catcher, right before starting the stride foot forward. This closing should occur at the time the pitcher is beginning to come towards home plate. Remember, if this is how the hitter chooses to prepare then make sure his weight begins more on the back leg because just closing the front shoulder will not get the hitter's weight back.

Drill # 14 – Hitch or Hand Load

This is a little more difficult but is very effective if done correctly. The hitters start the bat in an incorrect hitting position — like too low, too high, too forward or even flat. They move their hands and barrel to the correct position as they prepare to swing. As the hands move to the correct hitting position, the weight is on or moves to the back leg. The timing of this is crucial so that the hitters' hands are in the right position when it is time to swing the bat. Because more timing is needed with a hitch, most coaches think of this as a negative tendency. It isn't necessarily so, as long as the hitters can get the hands ready on time.

Flat bat start, trigger by bringing knob down.

Back to correct hitting position before the swing.

Drill # 15 – Knee Tuck

A lower-half trigger is done by tucking the front knee back towards the catcher as a way of preparing and beginning the stride forward. This is one of the more common and best loads because it will get the whole body ready. The one minor problem with this can be the timing factor. Lifting the knee requires precise timing, and as with the hitch it can be more difficult to get set on time, especially with the high knee lift. For this reason, it is best to lift the knee up and back just a few inches.

Remember, one of our keys is to have the hitter prepared and yet still as tension free as possible. The more relaxed the hitter can stay with his hands and stride up until the time to swing, the less important a trigger action. The relaxed hands and short steady stride will still allow the hitter to be quick and explosive. Some good hitters appear to not have a trigger action because of this ability to be relaxed and yet ready.

Starting position — back to hitting position.

Following are four other drills to help with preparation, "rhythm" and balance for the advanced hitter. These drills exaggerate the idea of getting the hitter ready but make a great point. Hitters who are not static and develop some movement with rhythm tend to be better hitters. Performing these drills while playing the hitter's favorite music can also help for developing a player's rhythm.

Drill # 16 – Rhythm Trigger Drill 1

The hitter will begin with the bat out in bunting position, but with both hands together and the weight on the front foot. As the pitcher begins to pitch the ball, the hitter starts the hands, weight and bat back to get ready to swing. The hitter should take normal batting practice using this drill. Over time the hitter should begin to get a feel for when and how to prepare for the pitch.

Hop forward.

Hop back to swing — rhythm drill to prepare bat.

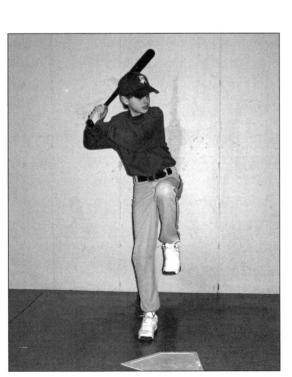

Exaggerated knee tuck to get weight back.

Drill # 17 – Rhythm Trigger Drill 2

With the bat relaxed on the shoulder, the hitter hops forward onto the front foot and then hops backward onto the rear foot and then takes the bat off the shoulder as the weight is on the back foot. The hitter then takes the stride and swing. The hitter should perform this drill on a tee.

Drill # 18 – Rhythm Trigger Drill 3

Have the hitter take an exaggerated front knee lift as the pitcher begins his move towards the plate. The hitter will look like the pitcher does when the pitcher lifts his knee in his windup. This will really force the hitter into getting his weight on the back foot and get him into a ready posi-

Walk behind drill — another fun drill to get ready and build up bat speed.

tion. You can have the hitter start wherever the bat is most comfortable with this drill. The hitter should not raise the whole body but only the front knee. If this drill is done with flips or regular batting practice, the coach should have the hitter lift the knee before flipping or pitching the ball.

Drill # 19 – Rhythm Trigger Drill 4

With this drill have the hitter back up a few steps towards the catcher. With the bat on his shoulder, the hitter walks towards the pitcher with the hitter's back foot walking behind the front foot. As the rear foot lands and the hitter begins the stride forward, the bat comes off the shoulder into ready position. This is the "Happy Gilmore" approach to hitting and is also very useful for hitters who are not aggressive. The hitter can actually take a little hop into the ball if more aggressiveness is desired. Just remember the rear foot goes behind the front foot on this drill, for this will serve to close the front shoulder. If the hitter takes the back foot in front of the front foot, the front shoulder will open.

- It is important for each hitter to find the method of preparation that suits her the best. No one way fits all, and each hitter must become comfortable with her method so that it happens naturally in the course of her preparation to swing. The development of a good preparation action will take time but can really pay off for the hitter in the long run.
- Personally, I liked to trigger by just lifting my front foot slightly up (slight knee tuck). Anytime I tried to trigger with the upper body it didn't feel comfortable and it was something that I continually had to think about. Remember, it has to become natural for the hitters so they trigger every time without thinking to do it.

Fundamental 8 – Stride Direction and Stay Back Drills

At this point we will have to break the drills into two parts. First will be stride direction drills. There are three possible problems here. First, there is stepping out or "in the bucket," which is very common for the young hitter. Second, there is the hitter who steps too much towards home plate or "dives" into the ball. The third problem is with the hitter who simply over-strides or appears to "jump" at the ball.

Later, I will talk about drills that will help the hitter wait on the pitch and "stay back."

1 Stride Problem – Stepping Out with Stride

The first thing to check is the hitter's head position. Make sure the hitter's head is turned toward the pitcher so that both eyes are facing the pitcher. If the hitter is not seeing the ball with the back eye, he may be stepping out to see the ball. Having the hitter start with a square stance as recommended above should allow the hitter to see the ball with both eyes.

Stepping out creates big problem for plate coverage and power.

For hitters who see the ball fine and still step out, I've found that the only real solution is to develop a greater use of the lead arm when hitting. If the lead hand and forearm do not fire towards the ball, many hitters step out to get the bat out front. This stepping out is *a major problem* and will only be fixed by using the lead arm correctly. Without the slight pull of the lead hand continuing into a karate chop action towards the ball, the bat will trail. Players whose bat trails will step out to get the bat out front. The following four drills are all good front-side drills that can eventually solve the stepping out problem.

Drill # 20 – Snap Towel Drill

Have the hitter get a dish towel and — with the lead arm only — use it to snap the towel at an object directly in front of him as if it was a pitch coming down the middle. It simply will not make sense to the player to not step and go directly at the object. I haven't had a hitter yet who would step away and try to snap the towel at the object. This will make the point for the hitter and will begin to show him how to use his front arm in order to attack the baseball.

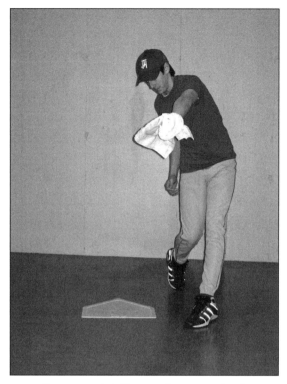

Snap towel drill — notice upper body position — in over the ball — excellent, Rob.

Lead arm swings to use front side and buildup lead arm strength.

Drill # 21 – Lead Arm Swings

Continuing with the same theme as the towel drill above, have the hitter use only his lead arm when hitting. The hitter should use a much smaller bat or choke way up on his bat so that too much strain is not put on their lead arm. The pull-pivot-push drill from the fundamental section is also a very effective lead arm drill. Some hitters will jump at the ball when performing this drill. If that is the case, have them do the drill with no stride.

As stated, using obstacles around the feet may make a good point about stride direction, but most hitters will continue to step out when the barriers are removed until they develop a good attacking front side.

Drill # 22 – Back Knee Pick Up

Another outstanding front-side drill, one that will be discussed later also, is the back knee pickup drill. As the hitters swing have them pick up their back knee, so that they come forward and towards the pitcher. You will notice that the only way hitters can pick the back knee up as they swing is to use their lead arm and hands to pull the bat towards the pitcher. Generally, the hitter will not be able to step out and still perform this drill. Once again, this is one of the great drills used to teach hitting and will be used for other problem remedies elsewhere in this book.

Back knee pick up — hips still open.

♦ As long as the hitter's back knee gets in front of the front leg on this drill, then the hitter will not be lunging. If the back leg is sliding behind him then he is not doing it correctly. It will serve to keep the front shoulder on the ball but without the correct hip rotation.

♦ Remember, hitting on a balance beam will force hitters to step directly, also, because they will have no choice if they want to stay on the beam as they should.

Drill # 23 – No Stride

This is another drill which can be used for multiple reasons and is employed by some major league hitters. It is called the "no stride" drill, which is pretty self-explanatory. The hitter simply does not take a stride but does everything else to prepare to hit. When the ball arrives the hitter takes his normal swing. This is a great teaching tool, for it eliminates any kind of false movements from the hitter's feet and will allow him to just work on his swing.

Sometimes coaches think that hitters who step out are scared of the ball, but in reality they don't understand correct hitting fundamentals. To young hitters it makes sense to step away in order to get the bat out front. Once they understand the right way and they begin to use their front side correctly, suddenly they no longer are afraid of the ball.

2 Stride Problem – Stepping (Diving) in Too Much

This habit is not all bad because it definitely keeps the front side closed and takes the hitter into the ball. The problem with stepping in too much is that the hips get locked up and they do not square up correctly. This will cause the hitter to have a tough time handling a good inside fastball. This diving in causes an early roll of the wrists, which causes a lot of balls to be hooked foul. This is one of the tougher habits to break but, again, it is not all bad. If the hitter can just take the step slightly more towards the pitcher and not into home, then the problem is usually solved.

The hips being unable to square up completely is often why a hitter may only be able to pull the ball at a young age. (The term "pull" means hitting the ball to the same side of the field as the side of the batters box that the hitter stands in). When hitters begin facing faster pitching they may be late all the time with this habit. The same inadequate results occur when they have a too-closed stance to begin with and don't square up with the stride. The chapter on "Problem Solving" will deal with this.

Drill # 24 – Stride Direction Barrier

The use of the balance beam or any safe barrier can be used to align the feet towards the pitcher. Setting the barrier in front of the front foot so that the hitter cannot step in too much will work. If the hitter dives in towards home, he will hit the barrier and realize the direction of his step.

Although I did not think using a barrier worked to solve the stepping-out problem, it is usually necessary for the diving-in problem.

Drill # 25 – Inside, Outside Tee

Another good drill for helping with the stride direction problem requires two batting tees. Place one on the outside corner and the other on the inside corner. Remember to stagger the tees appropriately so that the inside one is out front (towards the pitcher) and the outside one is back more. Have the hitter begin his stride, and as soon as his foot lands, the coach calls out either inside or outside pitch. Because the hitter doesn't know which ball to hit when he begins the stride, he should step the same on each pitch. The hitter should only hit the ball that is called with the correct swing and not both balls on the same swing. Hitting the ball in the direction of where it is located is the objective.

Use of the No Stride Drill #23 can also help. The hitter can square the hips with no stride, resulting in more balls hit to all fields.

3 Stride Problem – Over-striding

Most hitters will only stride to a balanced position because it is difficult to step to an out-of-balanced position. A good first move by the coach would be to *widen the hitter's stance* so that the same ending position is attained but the stride is much shorter. This will shorten the stride and allow the hitter to get the front foot down sooner with less movement.

Inside and outside pitch — step the same.

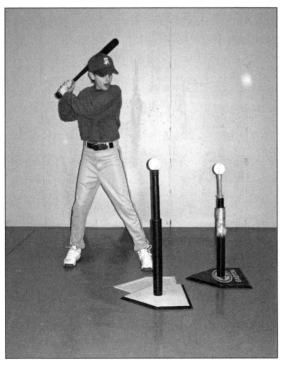

Learning to make contact on different pitch locations.

Don't over-stride, Jimmy.

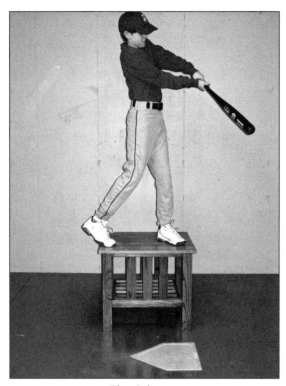

That's better.

Drill # 26 – Standing on Bench Drill

Have the hitters take their stance just a few inches from the end of a bench or the end of the balance beam. Have them take some strides. If they over-stride they will know it because they will fall off the bench. The coach can inject some fun and drive home the point by yelling "timber" as they fall.

Caution: The hitter should not take regular batting practice on the bench.

Drill # 27 – Obstacle in Front of Lead Foot

Place a heavy obstacle three to four inches in front of the lead foot. Obviously if the hitters attempt to stride too far they will hit the obstacle and be forced to stop their stride when they bump up to it.

◆ A brick is a good object to use as a barrier for it is firm enough so it won't give when the player hits up against it with their foot. The front of the balance beam works great for this also.

Another over-stride drill. Staying back, understanding head position while using hands.

◆ Barriers are good teaching tools because they will make the proper point and give instant feedback to the hitter. However, like many drills it doesn't always solve the problem when the barriers are taken away. I found that the best way to *control the stride* is to try to get the hitter a much more compact swing. More often than not a long swing created a long stride, so until the swing was shortened it was hard to control the stride. Shortening the swing will be discussed in the "Problem Solving" chapter.

◆ Hitting with no stride can solve all the stride problems. Some hitters may choose to hit in a game with no stride and it can work. If the hitter decides to hit with no stride, make sure they get the weight back and stay loose before swinging. Hitting with no stride, with two strikes can be especially good. The no stride approach certainly simplifies the lower half action and allows the hitter to just *concentrate on timing the ball.*

Staying Back

The second part of our stride discussion and drills involve "staying back." One of the biggest problems for many hitters, and probably the most mentioned problem for professional hitters is staying back. When a hitter does not stay back it means that they allow either their hands or their weight to drift forward before they really want to swing the bat. This usually will take away from any power or bat speed left in the swing and lead to a lazy swing. The causes of this not being able to "stay back" are usually one of three things:

1. The hitter gets overanxious and commits too early with their hands or their weight moving forward.
2. The hitter misreads the speed of the pitch and commits too early.
3. The hitter simply lacks confidence, which may be caused by a long swing or a weak and tired feeling that day.

Remember, staying back means the ability of the hitter to keep his hands and weight back until the ideal time to swing. This allows the hitter to coordinate throwing the bat and transferring their weight in a quick and explosive manner. In order to help solve this problem, the hitter must get the feel of the back side of his body generating more of the start of the swing. The following drills will help the hitter to stay back.

Remember the firing of the back knee Drill # 3 is good for staying back because it is difficult to fire the back knee if the hitter is not back to begin with.

Drill # 28 – On the Back Knee

Have the hitter take some swings on his back knee with the front foot out and the body facing the same as they would with normal hitting. This will give the hitter the idea and feel of staying behind the ball with the head and extending the arms and bat through the ball. Caution: Hitters should not take live batting practice while on their knee with hard baseballs because their ability to move out of the way is compromised.

Drill # 29 – Top Hand Hitting

Hitting with just the top hand on the bat will help to get the feel of staying back and using more of the back side to generate the start of the swing. Use of a smaller bat or choking way up on a regular bat is recommended for this drill. The hitter will feel the coordinated action of the back elbow and the rear hip. The hitters should hold their shirt with the lead hand so that they don't hit their free hand with the swing.

On back knee hitting will keep head back and make hitter use hands with good posture.

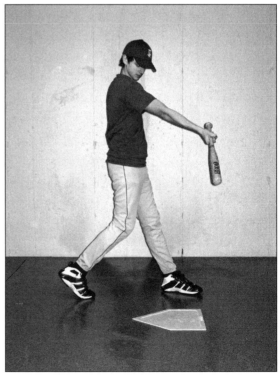

Top hand controls the barrel.

Drill # 30 – Hip Turns

The old fashioned hip turn drill will help the hitter understand how to open the hips. Have the hitter put the bat behind his back and just above hip level. With his hands on the bat the hitter then rotates the hips very fast and transfers the weight from the back leg to the front side. I like to have the hitter keep the hands on the bat as opposed to placing it in the arms. Although a little more uncomfortable for the hitter this method won't allow the bat to fly out when working on turning the hips.

Drill # 31 – Head Back

Set another bat on the ground in the middle of the hitter's feet when the hitter is in his stance. Have the batter take batting practice with the intention of keeping his head from drifting forward (towards the pitcher) of the bat. After each pitch have the hitter stop and look to see where his head is in relation to the bat. The head should stay even or move just an inch or two in front of the bat on the ground after the completion of the swing.

Hip turns and weight shift.

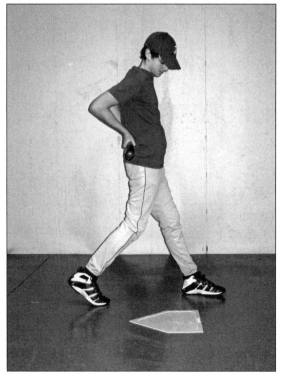

Using the lower half.

Drill # 32 – Net Close behind Hitter – Staying Back

This is a very good drill for getting the feel of staying back.

Have the hitter stand just slightly in front of a net. The net is where the catcher would be standing. After making contact with the ball our hitter tries to finish by hitting the back end of the cage. If they drift forward too far then they will have no chance of hitting the back net. The hitter should not pull their front shoulder to hit the net on the follow through though.

 This drill will be discussed again in the next section for another purpose.

Keeping head behind — throwing bat forward.   *Net behind drill for staying back and compact swing.*

Drill # 33 – Behind the Hitter Soft Toss

Another fine drill is to have the coach set up a few feet behind the hitter. Caution: The coach should make sure they are out of range of the hitter's bat on their follow through. As the hitter begins his step forward the coach will flip the ball forward into the hitting zone. It won't make sense for the hitter to lunge forward and not stay back with the ball coming from behind.

Fundamental #9 – Hitting Position

Fundamentals 1 through 8 and the associated drills are designed to achieve the great hitting position talked about in the fundamental chapter. The fake drills talked about in that chapter are the best way to work on making sure the hitter is in good hitting position. This is where the use of video analysis or a mirror are most helpful to show the hitter the position they are in when the front foot lands.

Head down, full turn and finish.

Behind hitter flips for staying back.

Fundamental # 10 – First Move

Remember, by first move we're talking about the break of the back knee and the pull of the lead hand.

- ◆ The fundamental Drills # 1 through 4 are all good for this first move.
- ◆ Another excellent drill for correcting the first move is the back knee pick up drill # 22. As mentioned there, this drill will force the hitter to begin the swing with the little pull of the bat with the lead hand towards the ball.

A few other drills that will help the "first move" are:

Missing net on swing forward for good first move and compact swing.

Drill # 34 – Net Close behind Hitter Version 2 – Compact Swing

Have the hitter stand in hitting position directly in front of a net. The net is behind him where the catcher would be. The hitter takes regular swings trying to avoid hitting the net on the way forward but hitting the net on the follow through. In order to miss the net on the way forward the hitter will have to throw his hands away from the net with that slight pull forward with the lead hand and with a compact motion. Having the hitters try to hit the net on the follow through insures that they do not lunge away from the net in order to miss it on the first move.

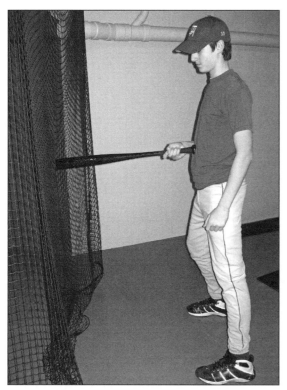 

Will force good hip turn and inside hands — no reaching drill.   *Just scrape end of net on swing.*

Drill # 35 – Net Drill to Avoid Reaching

With the net now directly in front of the hitter where home plate is, the hitter sets the knob of the bat at his belly button. The barrel end of the bat is just touching the net. The hitter should swing trying to just scrape the end of the bat along the net. This will also force the hips to open and create that inside pulling action necessary on the first move.

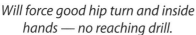 If the hitter is not hitting the net slightly then there is a good chance their front shoulder is pulling out. This is not desirable so the hitter should scrape the net slightly.

Drill # 36 – Tee behind hitter

Set a tee slightly behind the hitter towards the catcher and set it hip high. With flips or another tee set up in the hitting zone the hitter should come over the rear tee before making contact. Swinging over and missing the back tee is another way of developing a good first move in a direct and compact manner.

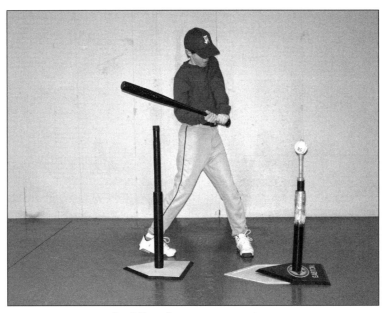

Avoiding the uppercut swing.

Fundamentals # 11 and # 12 – Swing Plane and Contact

The swing plane is what comes between the first move and contact. Doing the drills in the above section will put the bat on the correct swing plane. The tilt of the body at the waist will determine the actual plane that the bat moves on. If the first move is correct and contact position is correct the swing plane will be good.

Speaking of "swing plane," I try to teach the hitters that the swing is like an airplane landing. It involves the bat head (the plane) beginning a gradual descent until the plane levels off and remains on the runway as long as possible until it turns into the terminal. It's a good illustration for the young hitter.

Contact position is another one of those crucial positions in the swing but another tough action to work on because from start to finish the swing happens so fast. Reviewing Drills # 6 and 7 are great for working on this.

The next 3 drills will help with contact position also.

Drill # 37 – Pad under Back Elbow

The hitter places a pad under the back elbow. This will keep the hitter from casting the bat on the first move and will facilitate the correct palm up and palm down position at ideal contact. The hitter should allow the pad to fall out at extension. Remember, the back elbow will come down and very close to the rear hip with the correct swing. This will help the hitter get this feeling.

Drill # 38 – Modified Batting Practice

The coach will stand about 20 feet in front of the hitter and throws balls to the hitter. The hitter hits the ball back to the coach with a short half swing. To hit the ball directly to the coach the hitter will have to have the right hand position at contact. This is similar to the game of pepper which uses more players to field and throw pitches to the hitter.

Drill # 39 – Outside Pitch Tee Work

The correct hand position at contact can be achieved by working on driving the

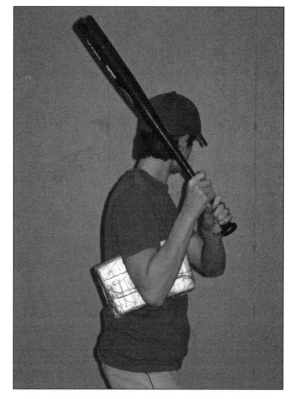

Avoiding the reach — staying inside the ball.

outside pitch to the opposite field. Set the tee on the outside corner and the hitter should hit the ball to the *opposite field*. If the wrists roll early the ball will not go to the opposite field.

This is easily done with short straight on flip work. The coach flips the ball on the outside portion of the plate. After the hitter gets a feel for this then the coach should flip the ball towards the middle and inside. If the swing was correct on the outside pitch then it should be correct on the middle and inside pitch. The point of contact will change for these two pitches but the hand position at contact is the same. The swing is correct on the middle pitch if the hitter is hitting the ball back through the middle. The swing will be correct on the inside pitch if the hitter is pulling the ball in fair territory or very close. If the swing is incorrect on this inside pitch the hitter will be hitting it way foul.

Outside pitch hand position for "perfect" swing.

Fundamentals # 13, # 14 & # 15 – Hip Action, Weight Shift & Head Position

Many of the drills listed previously will be working on these actions. If the previous actions are done correctly the hips and weight shift will take care of themselves, but these drills will help.

Drill # 40 – Freeze Balance Drill

After the completion of the hitters' swing have them hold their finish position and lift both feet alternately. If their weight is distributed well upon finish they should be able to lift each leg. If the hips opened correctly the hitter's bat should be around his back with the hitter's belly button facing the pitcher.

Drill # 41 – Head Down at Contact

Place an object just off to the opposite side of the hitter and out front of home a few feet. After the hitters make contact with the ball have them keep their eyes in the direction of the placed object before looking up. An empty soda can, a few baseballs or a fielder's glove works well for this. Another variation of this is to have the coach drop down a number of fingers after contact and have the hitter tell the coach what number of fingers. This can be done by the coach with tee work, flips or even regular batting practice. This is a good drill for helping the hitters to understand the fundamental of keeping their head down and their eyes on the ball.

Drill # 42 – Head Position Drill – Video

If the coach can film the hitter, put the thumb on the hitters head on the screen when he is in his stance. Keep the thumb in the same position throughout the swing and notice where the head is at contact and finish. If the head has traveled too far from the initial spot then this can be a source of the hitter's troubles. Ideally the head should stay very close to the start position throughout the swing.

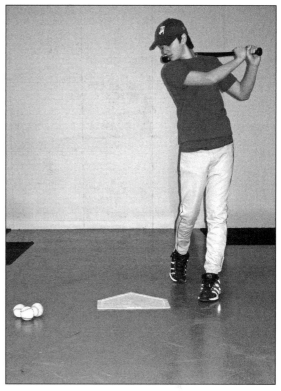

Head on ball to contact drill.

◆ Drills # 33, and # 43 below are good for keeping the head steady. The hitter should not pull the head if the ball is coming from behind and they will have to keep a steady head to do the rapid fire drill.

◆ Having the hitter hit on their back knee (Drill #28) is a good head stabilizing drill also.

◆ Remember, swings on a balance beam will reinforce many of these correct actions because if done incorrectly the hitter will not remain on the beam on completion of the swing.

Advanced Drills for Bat Speed

Drill # 43 – Rapid Fire

Either from the side or from behind a screen directly in front of the hitter, the coach will give the hitter 5 or 6 tosses in a row. The coach should allow the hitter just enough time to swing forward and back before flipping the next ball. This will require a quick rhythmic action by the hitter while maintaining balance and keeping the head in. Unfortunately, I've seen this drill done incorrectly many times.

It is important for the hitter to still take a full correct swing each time to finish. The coach can still isolate pitches all with the same location so the hitter is hitting the ball to the field where the ball is pitched. For example, the coach should give the hitter five pitches in a row on the outside of the plate for five shots to the opposite field. The drill will not be productive if the coach pitches so fast that the hitter cannot use his body and swing correctly. This is often referred to as a fast hands drill, but in reality it is forcing balance and hip action just as much. If the hips don't work and the balance is lost that will show up on this drill. This is a good drill to finish the workout with as it can be very exhausting.

Drill # 44 – Dropped Ball

In the chapter "Instant Feedback" this drill was # 8. It is such a good drill that it is repeated here. Remember, I recommend this drill over the side toss drill because it will

Dropped balls for quick swing and staying back.

force the compact swing. After the hitter strides, the coach can drop the ball immediately, which will mimic a fastball or hold the ball for a second or two and this will mimic the off speed pitch. Both ways force the hitter to wait and try to be quick. You can lower the height of holding the ball for the more advanced hitter. The higher the hitter can hit the ball after leaving the coach's hand, the better, quicker and more compact the swing is. The hitter obviously tries to hit a line drive before the ball hits the ground. If the hitter is taking the ball off their shoe tops, then put a tee slightly behind her at about hip high and this will eliminate the long swing.

All hitters have a *natural swing plane* which is the level that their swing normally comes through the hitting zone. This drill is a good way of finding that swing level. The hitters will generally try to hit the ball at the level of their natural swing. If the swing is long and the players are hitting the ball at the knee high level, they may have too long of a swing.

Drill # 45 – Self Flips

This is another drill that can help develop a quick, compact swing. Have the player hold the bat with only his lead arm and set the bat on the back shoulder. The hitter will hold a ball with the back hand and flip it up no higher than eye level out front in the hitting zone. Then the hitter grabs the bat with both hands and takes the normal swing, trying to hit line drives. If the hitter keeps the ball below eye level it will force the hitter to be very quick and develop stronger hands. This is

Self flips for developing bat quickness and good hands.

Remember Rob, flips should stay below eye level.

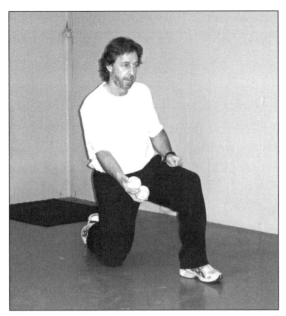

*Double ball flips for waiting,
discipline and quick bat.*

a tough drill at first because the player may have a hard time flipping good balls to hit. With time he will get the hang of it and he will feel it working his hands and forearms immediately. Remember, the ball should be flipped no higher than eye level. The more experienced player can even work on inside and outside pitches with this drill.

Drill # 46 – Two Ball Flips

This is another great drill for quickness. The coach is either off to the side or behind a screen in front of the hitter. The coach flips two balls at a time with the same hand. As the ball reaches the hitting zone, the coach yells out which ball to hit, either the high one or the low one. The coach can call out high or low or fast (high one) or curve (low one). In order to hit the ball the coach calls out, the hitter will have to wait till the last second to swing. Telling the hitter to hold up on pitches that you call that are not strikes is very challenging and helps to teach the strike zone.

A tip for the coach flipping the ball is to concentrate on flipping one of the two balls to the area you want to call out on that pitch. It isn't as hard to flip good pitches as you might think, but it does take practice to get good location with the pitches.

▶ *Final Thought* ◀

There are a lot of fun and challenging drills for developing hitters. Remember the drills the hitter finds the most difficult are usually the ones that will help the hitter the most. These drills will be used in the "Problem Solving" chapter of this book. Finally, a drill is only useful if it is done correctly!

6 | Teaching the Strike Zone

"Was the umpire pitching and struck you out or did you strike out?"

The year 1984 was going to be a make or break year for me. I was coming off a good year back in Triple A baseball with the Indians and was getting another shot at the major leagues with the Seattle Mariners. I had learned a few things from the first few times I was in the major leagues. Mainly, what I had done fundamentally at the plate up till then was not good enough. Secondly, the season was a long grind and it was important to maintain the physical and mental strength to perform consistently. Third, I had learned the hard way that I could not consistently get the sweet spot of the bat on the ball against major league pitching. It was important to try a new approach if I was going to have a chance to hang up in the majors. I decided to try choking up on the bat. Now this wasn't your normal half inch or so. This was a full fledged two and half to three inches up the bat. This action made all the difference because it allowed me to put the sweet spot on the ball much more often. It also made it easier for me to stay on top of the ball and eliminate many of the lazy fly balls that I had been hitting.

As a hitting coach I tried to convey this attitude to the hitters. Not necessarily to choke up, as it seems like that is a dirty word to most players nowadays, but to be willing to try different things and to learn to adjust. For each level that the player moves up, the pitchers improve and adjust to the hitters so the hitters must do the same. *It is almost always better to hit the ball on the sweet spot of the bat no matter how much you had to choke up than to not put the barrel on the ball. If I hit a ball solidly and the outfielder caught it, then I knew to choke up a little more so the ball would fall in front of the outfielder. My new theory paid off with 180 hits in 1984.*

Hitters need to keep an open mind to trying different things as long as they are based on good fundamentals. When things are going well, ride out the good streak, and when things are going badly, try to make some little adjustments and get back to work.

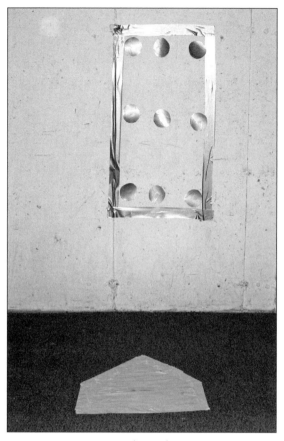

Learning the strike zone.

Teaching hitters to learn the strike zone just like learning the swing is an ongoing ordeal. This teaching should begin at an early age. The coach should not assume the hitter knows what the strike zone is because it tends to be called a little different at each level.

Asking the hitter what a ball is and what is a strike is important. This is most necessary at the younger ages. It is important that the coach takes nothing for granted even with the more experienced hitters. The coach should continually tell the hitters during batting practice to only swing at strikes even if the pitcher cannot seem to throw them. If a hitter swings at a pitch in practice that is not a strike point that out to him. Along the same lines, if the hitter takes a pitch in practice that is a strike but the hitter does not swing, ask him where he thought the pitch was. Tell him it is OK not to have swung but that it was a strike. This approach over time will usually pay off for the hitter with good discipline in the game.

If the umpire allows the strike zone to expand greatly as is common in young players' games, I still believe that the hitters should not chase pitches that are obvious balls. *Praise the hitter* for not swinging at an obvious bad pitch and tell them not to worry about it even if it meant a strike out. This approach will pay off as the hitter advances to higher levels of ball. The umpires will be more consistent as the pitching improves and the hitter's learned discipline will be a plus. Many coaches tell their hitters to swing at bad pitches because the umpire is calling them strikes. I don't believe this approach benefits the players in the long run. It is better to praise the hitter for not swinging at obvious balls and move on.

There are a few reasons why a hitter will chase bad pitches.

1. Hitters with a long swing will have to decide whether to swing sooner than hitters with a more compact swing. Over time hitters will have a sense of

timing on how long it takes them to get the bat out front. This may be somewhat subconscious but the hitters will know. Hitters with the long swing will begin their swing sooner, when the pitch may still look like a good pitch. If they could have waited longer they would have noticed that the pitch was not a strike. The best way to avoid swinging at bad pitches is to shorten the swing and this will allow the hitter to wait longer on the pitch. This will be especially helpful with learning to hit the curve and other off speed pitches. If the hitter cannot wait long enough he will continually get fooled on these pitches and chase them out of the strike zone.

2. Over-anxious hitters have a tendency to swing at bad pitches. This is most evident with two strikes on the hitter as they are fearful of the strike out. After the game or at practice, praise the hitter for being ready and willing to swing but keep reminding this type hitter to be more patient. This is a delicate area because you do not want to take the hitters aggressiveness away. As written in the "Mental Side of Hitting" chapter, the coach should simply keep reminding the hitter to see the ball.

Good hitters have a way of being *relaxed, ready and aggressive.* This can be learned over time. Two strike hitting requires a *heightened concentration level.* This also can be learned, but a relaxed readiness is mandatory to be a good two strike hitter.

Other ways to teach good plate discipline:
1. Have the hitter stand in the batter's box as a pitcher is warming up. Make sure the hitter is wearing a helmet and is prepared to get out of the way if the ball comes at him. It is best that the player does not have a bat in his hands in case he forgets and swings. Have the player just watch pitched balls and call out ball or strike. It is difficult often times to get enough practice with a pitcher so this is a great way to see more pitches at game speeds.
2. In batting practice, have the hitters watch any pitch they don't swing at all the way into the catcher's glove or past home plate if there is no catcher. Sometimes, the hitter will think that a pitch is a ball, but when he notices where the catcher caught the ball he will realize the pitch is a strike. This is a good habit to develop at all times.
3. A fun drill at practice is to put full gear on the players and have them stand behind the catcher and call balls and strikes as if they are the umpire. This will make them more aware of the strike zone also.

4.   Just like we have hitters visualize getting base hits it is important that they visualize themselves taking or laying off pitches that are not good to swing at. The discipline has to come from the mind first before it will translate into action. Visualization is the picture of an action in the player's mind before it happens and will be discussed in the chapter on the Mental Side of Hitting.

▶ *Final Thought* ◀

Having good plate discipline is a continual learning process. Keeping the hitter focused on just seeing the ball without distracting him with mechanical thoughts is very important. The coach must be careful of getting upset when the hitter swings at bad pitches because they do not want to have tentative hitters.

7 | Coach Talk – Constant Reminders and Adjustments

"Knowledge creates confidence — the good coach is the knowledge creator"

The coach is such an important person in the ball player's development. When I look back on my career, besides my parents, the coaches I had are the people I most looked up to in my life. Besides the technical help they provide, the confidence the coaches provide the player can be so important in developing one's character and future. My manager with the Seattle Mariners helped me immensely in this area. Being an average player at best I was always wondering if I belonged in the majors and manager Del Crandall was there many times for me.

During spring training of 1984, I was again battling to make the big club. Crandall must have noticed that I was pressing somewhat and he told me to relax that I was to be his second baseman for the coming season. What a relief. The confidence he showed in me made all the difference and I went on to have a fine year with a .294 batting average.

Another time I was mired in a 0 for 26 slump and was worried about being benched. I showed up and noticed I was starting and leading off that night. Once again, the confidence the manager showed made me want to perform well and help us win. Luckily, I had three doubles in the game that night and it was on to the next game.

Along with the player's parents, the coach should be a great source of confidence. Coaches are role models and their actions and influence will mold the players for a long time.

Most pitchers at a young age get very uptight about hitting batters with a pitched ball. Because of that they generally will try to keep the ball away from the hitters on the outer portion of the plate. Also, with aluminum bats pitchers are taught to keep the ball away from hitters as much as possible. For these reasons and more, as you will read about, hitters need to work on hitting the outside pitch as much as possible.

Over the years of teaching hitting and during the lessons I gave, there were certain statements that seemed to always be repeated. Some spoke to the common breakdowns in the hitter's mechanics. Others dealt with a hitter's mind set, approach or "game plan" for hitting. Some of the statements are just a different way of saying the same thing about a particular aspect of hitting. Some may seem like common sense but once again, the good coach will assume nothing. Here are the most frequent quotes and an explanation of each.

1. **"Balance comes from your head so keep your head in over the ball."** When I would ask hitters where their balance comes from, there were many replies but almost never would the head be mentioned. In reality, the key to good balance when hitting is the head. The head should be leaning in towards home plate and this will correctly put the weight over the balls of the feet. It is important to maintain this head position throughout the complete swing. A good hitter will feel like his head is almost over the ball at contact, at least on inside pitches. To *see the ball hit the bat at contact*, it is necessary to have the head in the correct position and good balance will follow.

Towel drill — Lead arm work and head down — good weight transfer.

2. **"Square up your stance so you can square up your hips at contact."** Remember, a square stance means that the toe line is on a parallel line directly towards the pitcher. This even stance gives the hitter the easiest and best chance to open the hips correctly into the swing. Teach your hitters to keep it simple and stay square with their set up stance.

   Most hitters I've seen with a closed stance will usually do one of two incorrect moves when they start too closed. They will either stay closed with their stride and get locked up when they try to open their hips or step out with their stride in order to see the ball better and thus pull away from the ball.

The opposite from a closed stance, the open stance, has gotten popular over the last few years. Most young hitters that begin with the open stance will not step back into the ball correctly and therefore they are at a disadvantage. If a particular hitter has trouble seeing the ball from the pitcher's hand with a square stance, then this is one of the only reasons to have the open stance. It's OK to try different stances, but I've noticed that it is usually a desperate move when the real problem is with the swing and not the stance.

3.   **"The game wasn't designed so the pitcher can throw the ball by you, so stay back and trust your swing."** Many hitters get anxious at home plate and jump at the ball or commit too early on pitches. As a hitting coach it is important to convince the hitter to wait and not to commit to swing until the last possible moment. When taking batting practice, the coach should continually change speeds, starting with slower pitches until the hitters feel comfortable with waiting for the ball.

4.   **"Pick the ball up from the pitcher's hand and see it the whole way."** This may seem obvious but many hitters do not track the ball completely the entire distance from the pitchers hand to the hitting zone. As mentioned in the above point # 3, it is correct to teach the hitter to wait for the ball. However, I've seen many hitters learn to wait too long because they are not concentrating on timing the ball the whole way from the pitcher's hand. It is important to wait to make the final decision on whether to swing but the *hitter must time the ball the whole way.* Many good hitters will check their swing a lot and this is a good thing because they are timing the ball from the hand and are ready to swing if it is their pitch. Good timing will only be maintained if the hitter watches the ball each third of the way home and plans on hitting it until the last possible moment when they may hold up.

5.   **"The correct setup after the foot lands gives you a chance to be a good hitter — the *correct first move* after the stride foot lands *will make* you a good hitter."** This was discussed in the fundamental section of this book. Remember, if the hitter is not in the correct position when it is time to start the swing then he does not have a chance of being a good hitter. Once that is correct it is still mandatory that the first move towards the ball is correct in order for the hitter to be able to hit a variety of pitches. As a hitting coach, concentrating on the hitting position and this first move is important. The hitter's natural hand and eye co-ordination will then take over.

6. **"Remember the sequence – stride, hips, hands and barrel."** Many hitters will attempt to do too many things at once. The result is usually one of three things. First, they will step and swing at the same time. Second, they will start the swing with their upper body and not the lower body (a lunging action). Third they will cast the barrel to the ball and not allow the hands to lead the way. All three of these are incorrect, thus the reminder to stay back and remember the correct sequence of actions

7. **"Stay back with your stride not with your swing."** It is important to stay back with the hands and weight with the stride. When a good hitter swings though, everything goes to the ball except the hitter's head. The hands throw the barrel and the weight transfers into the swing towards the ball. Many average or below average hitters will stay back but then do not let everything go towards the ball with their swings. It should be a very aggressive action into the ball.

8. **"A long swing produces a long stride."** This may seem backwards but many hitters develop long swings and try to make up for them with long strides. As a hitting coach, I learned to treat the swing first and then the stride will begin to shorten up to a more manageable length. As the swing becomes more compact, the hitters will realize they have more time to *wait and stay under control* with the stride.

Hands-on approach the best.

9. **"You're losing the barrel — use your hands."** Many hitters are arms swingers and do not use their fingers, hands and muscles around the wrists enough. It is important for the hitter to use these speed muscles in the hands in order to achieve maximum bat speed and to control the barrel, especially on the first move. I tell hitters that the only muscles that should get tired when they hit are the hands and fingers. When you watch the all star home run derby contests, it's the hitter's hands that may become tired and thus not produce as many long balls. The big arm and leg muscles should not get tired very easily.

10. **"Stay behind and inside the ball."** Good hitters will keep their heads back and propel the bat forward. At the same time they will not reach for it. In order to get to the proper hand position at contact, the hands will stay close to the body as they swing. Good hitters will try to hit the inside back of the ball on all pitches. If the hands stay inside the ball, the hitter will take the outside pitch to the opposite field and will hit the inside pitch fair to the pull side.

Coach Talk – Mental Thoughts & Adjustments

11. **"Know what pitches you like best and look for them early in the count."** Remember, the hitter doesn't have to swing at any strike until there are two strikes on them. Good hitters lay off the pitches they don't hit well until the count dictates they have to swing at the tough ones. Hitters need to know which pitches they hit best. A good coach should help the hitters find out which pitch or pitches they hit best and then have them look for those pitches early in the count. Good hitters are willing to get behind in the count with the hope of getting their pitch, knowing that this is more important then swinging at any strike.

    This idea is great for the advanced hitter. For a youngster who is too selective or hesitant to swing the bat the opposite approach may be better. "Go up hacking" as they say.

12. **"Take the ball where it wants to go."** This is another way of telling the hitter to hit the ball where it is pitched. Good hitters will use the whole field when they hit. Bad hitters use the whole field when they hit. What? That's right. The difference is the good hitter will hit inside pitches to their pull side and outside pitches to the opposite field. Bad hitters will do the opposite. They will be late on the inside pitches and hit that one to the opposite field and will go out and hook the outside pitch to the pull side of the field. The chances of hitting the ball with much authority will definitely decrease with this latter type of hitting because the "power" hand position at contact will not be achieved.

13. **"Foul balls can be your friends."** A lot of hitters get upset when they foul balls off. Unless the ball was pitched in the hitter's ideal hitting zone, the hitter should treat the foul ball like a positive accomplishment. Some pitches

are better off being fouled off because they were not in an area where the hitter could hit the ball hard anyway. Obviously, if the hitter fouls off a very hittable pitch then that is different, but on tough pitches a foul ball will keep the hitter alive for possibly a better next pitch. Every hitter has certain pitches that they hit better than others but, generally, tough pitches are ones that are on the corners of the plate or at the upper and lower sections of the strike zone. Hitters with good swings will foul off tough pitches with two strikes and stay alive for another pitch. They are not intentionally hitting foul balls but their swing is good enough to get a piece of the tough pitches. Hitters that do not have as fundamentally correct swings would miss these tough pitches much of the time.

14. **"Location determines where you hit the ball not the speed."** Here we go again — another way of trying to get the hitter to understand good fundamental hitting. Many hitters will constantly pull slow pitching and be late on good fast pitching when the *location should be the key to where it is hit,* regardless of the speed. This should be especially stressed in batting practice so that the hitter keeps good timing and works on hitting the ball where it is pitched. At batting practice speeds it is usually easy to pull the ball solidly no matter where it is pitched, but this usually will not help the hitter's overall timing and swing with game speeds. The coach should point out to the hitters where they are hitting the ball in relation to where the ball was pitched.

15. **"If you can do it on the slow pitch then you can do it on the fast — you just have to react quicker."** Fundamentally, to hit the ball where it is pitched on a very slow pitch is just as difficult if not more so than a fast pitch. This is because the hitter must wait and remain in good hitting position till the last possible second. Many young hitters dislike slow pitchers and many older hitters dislike off speed pitchers. Once again, it takes a very good fundamental swing to hit slow pitching on the sweet spot of the ball and bat. Once a hitter can do this they are ready to work on faster pitching. Oftentimes I would just lob the ball at the hitters until they could hit *consistent line drives* back through the middle. Once they could wait and control the bat then I would increase the speed of pitches.

16. **"It takes perfect fundamentals to take the outside pitch and drive it to the opposite field."** To hit the ball to the opposite field on the outside pitch, the hitter must wait until the exact right moment and have the correct hand position at contact. Everything has to be timed just right. Once a hitter has

the correct swing on the outer half pitch, then the swing is almost always correct on the middle and inside pitches. The hitter just needs to hit the ball out front more on these latter pitches. A foul ball to the opposite side may be the result with the outer half pitch but this still may be the correct swing. In order to get their timing and swing back when in a slump, major league hitters will usually work on hitting balls to the opposite field until they get consistent doing this. As was mentioned earlier also, pitchers will tend to pitch to the outside of the plate so it is the pitch to get as proficient as possible at hitting. Also, as mentioned it is OK to foul it off.

17. **"It's OK to pull the ball but not OK to try and pull."** There is nothing wrong with pulling the ball but if the hitter tries to pull they usually will start to pull off the ball. This will cause a loss of timing and a hitting slump will follow. The hitter will also become vulnerable to outside pitches, curveballs and slower pitches if they are thinking or trying to pull the ball. Good hitters who want to pull the ball will attempt to hit the ball out front of home more without pulling off the ball with the front side. This is usually easier said than done so it doesn't usually pay to try and pull all pitches.

18. **"I'd rather have my B swing and swing at good pitches then have my A swing and chase bad pitches."** Obviously, there is no substitute for a good mechanical swing but it is not possible to keep the perfect swing day in and day out. However, *the hitter can swing at good pitches consistently.* It will be much easier to hit the ball solidly by swinging at good pitches. No good hitters hit tough pitches consistently well (except maybe a Vlad Guerrero).

19. **"With two strikes look away and adjust in."** With two strikes the hitter is trying to put the ball in play and avoid the strike out. (It is tough in this day and age to get hitters to choke up on the bat with two strikes, but this method can help.) Looking for the ball out over the plate will keep the hitter's front side closed as long as possible and protect against the outside and off speed pitches. This may make the hitter a little vulnerable on the inside fastball but hopefully the hitter will be quick enough to at least foul off the inside pitch.

20. **"With two strikes all hitters are the same — if the pitch is close, swing. What you do before you get to two strikes is what makes you a good hitter."** I try to tell hitters that the pressure is off when they have two strikes because then they have to swing if the pitch is a strike or even close to a strike. They usually don't believe me because nobody likes to strike out and that is definitely a danger with two strikes. The point to be made, though,

is that good hitters make *good decisions earlier in the count* so that they get their pitch to hit. When good hitters get their pitch they take advantage of it. Good hitters will learn to lay off tough pitches early in the count but to always be ready for their pitch.

21. **"You may not know what you are doing wrong but the fix is in the work."** This is pretty obvious but it's still important to keep reminding the hitter. Generally, it's best to be proactive when the hitter is struggling and take more swings and practice. As has been mentioned, a coach can tell you many times over what you are doing wrong but just knowing doesn't mean you can fix it without the correct muscle memory work. Also, it is good to remember that it is better to take twenty very good fundamental swings than it is to take one hundred swings that may be reinforcing the same bad habit. If the hitter is reinforcing bad habits the work may be counter productive. Stay with some good, sound fundamental drills as found in this book and it will usually pay off.

▶ *Final Thought* ◀

I once read that the one thing that good coaches have in common is that they are constantly talking and providing information. Many times the coach is repeating the same things over and over again with the hope that the players will adopt these repeated thoughts into their actions. I believe that if the coach can keep repeating these instructions in different ways, the players will not tune the coach out and these concepts will become ingrained in the player's minds.

8 | Mental Side of Hitting

"See the ball, hit the ball"

As mentioned earlier, my play in 1982 was subpar. In the off season, before the 1983 season, I came across a book on the mental side of sports. It actually had to do with tennis but the mental conditioning aspect of the book applied to any sport. This book definitely helped to turn my career around. The book taught me how to really focus in game situations. Many big time athletes talk about being able to "slow the action down" in their minds. I discovered what they meant, and all of a sudden 90 mile per hour fastballs didn't seem as intimidating as they once were.

I applied these ideas to my season in Triple A ball in 1983 and went on to win the batting championship in the American Association that year. I remember on separate occasions catchers asking me how I could continually not swing at certain close pitches. It was like the ball was in slow motion at times. I actually felt like the legendary Ted Williams with how well I was seeing the ball.

Often the coach thinks that some players have "it" and others don't, the "it" being a baseball sense or "instincts." The ability to focus is something that players can work on and improve. Players can have better games with the increased ability to focus. The result will be a better sense of accomplishment. The coach should help with this by trying to keep the players' heads in the games and their "eyes on the ball."

This is the area where things can be very difficult for a hitting coach. Obviously we want our hitters to be smart but we don't want them to think. That's right. Good hitters have a subconscious feel for what needs to be done and are able to concentrate only on the ball. For good hitters it is mandatory to be able to put all of their concentration on the ball during the game. Practice is when a hitter can think, make adjustments and work on different aspects of hitting. All the swing thoughts that

I hope they are listening.

the coach is teaching in the chapter on "Coach Talk" need to be internalized in the hitter's subconscious so that they just happen over time. Good hitters will start to adapt those swing thoughts into their normal thought process and, along with good fundamentals, will have the opportunity to be very successful. *Games are for trusting the swing* and concentrating on just seeing the ball. When you hear of hitters or athletes being "in the zone" this is what is meant. They have the ability to store all their good habits and thoughts in the back of their mind and only concentrate on the here and now of the ball coming towards them. The ability to get the hitter in the zone as often as possible is the goal of the good hitting coach.

You may have noticed that many of the statements made in the chapter on "Coach Talk" dealt with the mental approach. Remember, practice time is where the physical and mental side is taught. Not all players have the natural instincts that others have, but the mental side can be learned and improved upon, although good hitters do not think they do have a *plan* when they go up to home plate. Good hitters know which pitches they hit best and which pitches they have trouble with. Using this knowledge, they will go up to home seeing the ball and planning on only swinging at certain areas or zones early in the count. As mentioned in the chapter on "Coach Talk" all hitters are the same with two strikes. What makes or breaks most at-bats is what the hitter decides to do before they get to two strikes. Hitters should know their own strengths and weaknesses, and this should determine what their plan is for that at-bat. For instance, hitters who pull the ball better should look for pitches they can pull, and high ball hitters should look for higher pitches.

Early in the count is when a hitter can "zone" in or "guess" with the pitcher. The term zone means that the hitter will look for a pitch only in a particular location. The hitter who is looking for a ball in a particular zone will only swing if the ball is in this area. The concept of guessing refers to the type of pitch. The hitter will guess that the pitcher will throw a particular pitch (e.g., curveball) on the next delivery. With two strikes the hitter has to adjust to what the pitcher is throwing. This is another reason why hitting in the big leagues can be easier. The pitchers are so good that the hitters often times know where the ball will be pitched. The tough part is that the pitcher usually knows the weak spot in the hitter's swing and will try to exploit it. The hitters who learn to adjust the best and have the fewest weak spots are the most successful.

There are many mental obstacles that can get in the way of being an effective hitter. Let's explore some of these and see what can be done about it.

1. **Fear** – This is far more prevalent in the young hitter — especially one that has been hit a few times at a young age. The ball does hurt and nobody likes pain.
   Solution
   a) It's important to try to have the hitter expect every pitched ball to be over the middle of the plate. Before pitching the ball, ask the hitter where he expects the ball and make sure he says over the middle. Then throw it and see how he reacts. If it comes at him teach him how to get out of the way, usually by turning away from it or ducking.
   b) A good batting machine can be useful because it will pitch consistent strikes and the hitter can hit without fear of the ball coming at him. Try to have them keep the same aggressiveness and thoughts when they are in a game as when they are in the batting cage.
   c) Use of a *softer ball* when pitching to the hitter can help. Tennis, whiffle and rag balls are great and the hitter will feel more comfortable facing these balls. Hopefully, with time the hitter will overcome his fear.

   ◆ This was mentioned in the "Advanced Drills" chapter but it bears repeating. The coach should be careful of mistaking stepping away from home with fear of the ball. I've had many students whose parents thought their child was scared of the ball when in reality they just did not understand the correct fundamentals. Many of these students think that to get the bat out to the ball it makes sense to step out. This can be corrected with some good fundamental front side drills.

◆ Repetition and practice can *reverse fear,* and *no player is beyond hope.*

◆ Finding coach pitch or machine pitch leagues at the younger age can certainly help in this matter.

2. **Nervousness** – This is a common symptom for hitters of all ages. Many parents express that their young hitter gets too nervous. It is important to explain to the hitter that nerves are normal and can be a good thing because they get the adrenaline and energy going. Convince the hitter that they can only use this energy if they concentrate through it by watching the ball better. Putting all their concentration on the ball will eliminate the ability to think about the nerves. The best way to relax a little is to have the hitters take a deep breath before getting in the batter's box. I know this sounds simple but the hitter needs to realize that even big leaguers get nervous. The big leaguer, for the most part, has learned to concentrate on the here and now to use the nerves in a positive way. Another thing that might help is something my mother always told me to do out on the field — "smile". This is a hard thing to do if one is too nervous, so getting the youngsters to smile can really break the tension.

3. **Parental Pressure and Fear of Failur**e – Another common feeling is the pressure to do well. All kids want to please their parents, and when they do not perform well they think that they are letting their parents down. All athletes have a fear of failure, some more than others. The more pressure the parent puts on the player the greater the fear of failure. Too much fear of failure will lead the player to feel like it is not worth playing anymore. This pressure, fear of failure and not wanting to play anymore can put a huge strain on a relationship and one that I've seen last for years.

    Unfortunately, the hitters themselves cannot alleviate this pressure. The parents have to ease up somewhat. This is a delicate area but if the parents seem approachable, then the coach can mention something to the parents about how tense their son or daughter is playing. Maybe the parents will get the idea that the pressure is coming from them. As mentioned earlier in this book, all parents are their child's coach so it is important that they follow the guidelines outlined in the chapters on "Having Fun" and "Be the Coach You Were Meant to Be."

A sign that a player is trying to please their parents too much is when they are constantly looking in the stands at their parents instead of concentrating on the action. It is important for parents to be supportive of their child's endeavors but it is necessary that they do not make their performance too important. It may be necessary for the parents to take a game off from time to time or to watch the game from a distance.

Parents should remember that the good natured environment that they present immediately after the competition is the key. It is important for parents to judge the *effort* and not the results. It is important for kids to realize that they are so much more than how they perform on a playing field. The parent's first question after a game should be, "Did you have fun?" If the player gets very defensive over questions about their performance, it is best to change the subject and visit the performance at a later time. Easier said than done sometimes, but it is usually worth it.

4. **Self Pressure** – Some players put too much pressure on themselves. Hitting is a tough art for the players who put a lot of pressure on themselves. As a youngster moves up in levels the competition will improve to the point where the hitter will make more outs than hits. Some players have a difficult time with failure. A good coach will constantly try to teach this type of player the art of patience and the nature of the game. Some of my most frequent comments to the hitters are:

    a) "Your goal is not to prove anything to anyone but to improve."
    b) "Don't worry about hits — try to have as many quality at-bats as possible. A quality at bat is putting good swings on hittable pitches."
    c) "You are one swing away from putting it all together, and since you don't know when that swing may come, stay positive."
    d) "Remember your good at bats and forget the bad ones or this game will drive you nuts."

5. **Confidence (or a lack of)** – This is a huge part of hitting. The number one job of the good hitting coach is to try and develop confidence in each hitter. Here are some things the coach can do for a hitter.

    a) Try to get them to believe in their swing.
    b) Keep reminding them of a nice hit they had — preferably in a game or in practice if needed.

c) Put each player in game situations during hitting practice so that when the situation occurs in the game they will have been there before and will be more prepared.

d) Tell the hitter that they remind you of a certain big league hitter.

e) Don't teach mechanics in the game. Remember that is what practice is for.

f) Keep reminding them to believe in themselves. There will be times when no one will believe that they will get a hit, but tell them to always believe in themselves.

g) If a player seems to be losing confidence, in a positive way give them something they should try before the next game. Keep the idea as simple as possible and even make up something if you are not sure what is wrong. As long as the hitter has some hope for tomorrow then all confidence will not be lost.

h) Let them know that you are pulling for them.

i) Praise the hitters for the good at-bat even if it doesn't lead to a hit.

j) Keep the hitters focused on never "giving up an at bat." This means the hitter should stay focused no matter what the score of the game is and no matter what the results of the hitter's previous at-bats. Many hitters will get down after making an out or two and be mentally defeated before their next at-bat.

Signs That a Hitter's Confidence Is Affected

It is important for the coach to watch for signs that the hitter is losing or has lost confidence. Some of these are as follows:

1. The player's body language and facial expressions are the most obvious. If the hitter is hanging their head or appears disgusted, then this is the most obvious sign that a player's confidence is waning. Any change in the player's normal behavior may be a sign also. Hitters who would rather bat near the end of the batting order than at the top of the order generally are short on confidence and may need a boost in confidence.

2. A loss of aggressiveness at the plate. This usually will show up in a number of ways:

    a) The hitter simply will not swing the bat. They seem to be always looking for a walk.

b) The hitter takes a pitch right down the middle and then proceeds to swing at the next pitch no matter where it is located.

c) The hitter will only swing when behind in the count. These hitters want to be forced to swing the bat so they wait until they are in counts where they have to swing. This usually is with two strikes on the batter.

d) The hitter who goes up and swings early and often. This one can fool you. Some hitters are so afraid to strike out that they will go up to home and swing at anything and everything so that they don't get into a two strike count. Talk to this type hitter about looking for a better pitch early in the count but tell them you admire their aggressiveness.

Here are some things that a coach should not do.

a) The coach should not overwhelm the hitters with instruction and with too many things to work on.

b) Don't ignore any team member — especially the weaker hitters. Feeling ignored by the coach may feel worse than being yelled at.

c) Don't show disgust by looking away or rolling the eyes when the hitter doesn't perform the way you want.

d) Don't let the player blame their bad at-bat on the umpire. Rarely does the ump blow all three strikes that the player gets.

e) Don't give false praise. There is a fine line between staying positive and giving false praise. Most players will recognize when they are getting false praise, and they may start to tune the coach out. Saying "hang in there" is better than "you did great" when the player had an obviously rough day.

▶ *Final Thought* ◀

Each player brings a different mental state to the field. It is important for the coach to recognize the various confidence levels of their players and adjust their coaching appropriately. Just as each player develops physically at different rates, they develop their mental side at differing rates.

Hitter's Agenda for a Good Mental Approach

Some of these ideas will be too advanced for the young hitter. The good coach should help with some of these preparations.

1. There is no substitute for a good fundamental swing. All the confidence in the world will not overcome fundamentals that are not sound. The off season is a great time to work on the fundamentals and a great time to improve enough to pass up the competition. Study pictures, watch baseball on the television, rent instructional videos, go to camps and take lessons.

2. Spring training – Up the work load a few weeks before the start of games. This is the time to get mentally tough and get the "eye of the tiger" for the ups and downs of the season ahead.

3. Visualization starts the night before the game – Visualization is the reviewing in one's mind the action that will occur in the game. A hitter will actually see himself facing the pitcher, hitting a line drive, taking a close pitch, coming up to bat with the game on the line and winning the game, etc.

4. Pre-game – This is the time to get focused. The hitter should fine tune the swing with a drill or two on the batting tee or with some flip drills. The hitter should concentrate on one or two of the drills that work on the particular problem area that has been occurring of late. Follow up with a focused batting practice, concentrating on hitting the ball to all fields.

5. Immediately before the game try to observe what the pitcher is throwing (speed of fastball, off-speed pitches, release point, etc.). The coaches should be helping with this input.

6. Keep an eye on how the pitcher is pitching other hitters in the lineup, especially hitters similar to you.

7. On-deck circle – Try to get the rhythm and speed of the pitcher as you are getting loose swinging the bat. The hitter should not be surprised by the speed and pitches of the particular pitcher if they were *paying attention in the on-deck circle* and on the bench.

8. Final visualization – While walking up to home, the hitter should visualize himself hitting to a particular location in the field. Seeing it, believing it — the hitter will be surprised how often it happens. The situation may call for something besides just hitting. The situation may call for a bunt, a hit and run or a sacrifice fly. The intelligent hitter should visualize performing whatever action the coach may call for.

9. At-bat – The hitter should now "Clear the Mechanism" as was said in the movie "For Love Of The Game." Clear the mind of all thought and focus on the ball. All the preparation work from the off season to this moment will take over. Be satisfied knowing that you did all you could do to be successful for that at-bat.

10. Post-game analysis – Analyze the results — The number one question is, Did I swing at the right pitches? If the answer is no then that may be the problem right there. Be determined to make better decisions the next game. If yes is the answer then what were the results?

11. Back to the drawing board – Back to the tee, cages, live hitting or whatever to correct the problems and to be prepared for the next game when it starts all over again.

12. No regrets – You've done the work and prepared the best you could. You swung at good pitches and the hits didn't come. Keep your head up knowing that whatever the results you did your best and won't have to look back wishing you had done something else.

▶ *Final Thought* ◀

Serious ball players should work on their game skills about nine months out of a year. It is good to take a break for about three months in order to refresh both physically and mentally. When exactly players take the break will usually be determined by their other sporting activities. When players are away from the game, this is a great time to work on getting physically stronger and faster with weights. I always found this time to be great for mentally preparing for the season. When lifting weights I wasn't thinking about how I was going to look on the beach but rather how it was going to help my hitting during the season. The disadvantage of baseball players in the northern states is that the number of days that they can play baseball outside are numbered. The advantage is they have a built-in break time where they can take a break, refresh and prepare for the next season.

9 | **Problem Solving**

"You don't need to know what is wrong but you do need to know how to fix it"

Everyone remembers their first hit. I was with the Los Angeles Dodgers in 1980 and was excited and obviously nervous for my first appearances at the big league level. I put good wood on the ball in my first major league hit. Unfortunately, it was a bunt on a suicide squeeze play. Being so nervous at the time I don't really remember it that well. The pitcher charged in and I popped it up over his head in front of the second baseman and proceeded to beat it out for my hit. Besides being congratulated for my first hit, many players thought that I bunted it there on purpose and said good job. Actually it was just luck but I took credit for it anyway. Not having any power at all, I took much pride in my ability to bunt to get on base. It was a great feeling to bunt for a base hit, especially knowing that the defense was looking for it.

It's important for players to analyze their tools in order to best determine how they can help the team and their future. A coach can help each player to understand the areas that the player does well at and the areas that need more work. The coach must try to help the player use their individual talents to be the type of player they should be.

Getting a hitter out of a slump is never easy. The only way I know to do it is to get back to the basics and put in the work. Many slumps seem to occur right after a very hot streak. Sometimes it's just the law of averages catching up with them. Other times the hitter becomes too confident and forgets about performing the little things that go into a good fundamental swing. It was very common to have a hitter come back for lessons about three weeks into the season and say, "I started out great but have struggled the last few games." It is common before the season to be working on batting tees and drills that adhere to the fundamentals. However, when games begin the hitter tends to get away from these drills and the fundamentals can start to deteriorate. The next thing you know the hitter is not getting enough positive swings and a slump occurs.

It can be very difficult for even the best hitting coaches to figure out what a hitter may be doing wrong in a game situation. The distance the coach is away from the hitter, and the limited swings they may get from at-bat to at-bat, make this a difficult task. In batting practice there is the repetition of swing after swing so it is easier to analyze the hitter's mechanics. In a game though, the coach doesn't have this luxury of constant repetition. In the major leagues every at-bat is filmed and can be immediately analyzed. This is not a usual convenience for the lower levels. The coach should film the hitters once in a while in a game situation and have a qualified coach analyze the film. Often, the swing that a player produces in a game is totally different from his practice swing for whatever reason. Because of this difference, it is important to film her game swing and review it. The saying "the video won't lie" is true. Thus, filming can be a great teaching tool for the players (and anyone looking to learn more about hitting, for that matter).

As mentioned, it is difficult at most levels to be able to film and analyze the hitter's swing very often. Also, I don't recommend filming too often for young players as it can tend to put too much pressure on them to look good every time they are up to bat. So, without the use of constant video analysis, the hitter's at bats still need to be monitored in order to figure out what might be going right and wrong. What is important is that the coach or parent looks for the *tendencies* in the results of the hitter's at-bats. Is the hitter striking out too much? Are they hitting too many ground balls or pop ups? Are they pulling everything or always late? The results of the hitter's at-bats can give *clues* as to what is going wrong and then a game plan can be drawn up for how to fix the problem. If there are no major negative tendencies and the player is making good contact but not getting hits, then they might just be running into a string of bad luck.

Figuring out what may be wrong is not an exact science. If you ask five different people what the hitter is doing wrong you may get five different answers. As you know, when a hitter struggles there will be a lot of people who will try to help. They all mean well but it can be overwhelming and confusing to the hitter. "Try this, try that." Pretty soon the hitter doesn't know what to do and will take no confidence into the next game. This is where having a personal hitting coach or someone that really knows hitting, and one the hitter trusts, can be valuable.

In this section I will identify the problems which show up while hitting in games and the possible cause of why this result occurs. Then I will suggest some actions and drills that can help the hitter get back on track. Unfortunately, this can be a *trial and error* process but with a little work the players can usually snap out of their slumps. The main thing is that the players can do something about their struggles, and therefore it can give them some hope and confidence for the next game. Having *hope and confidence* is crucial in order to break out of a slump.

Some coaches can tell the hitter what they are doing wrong but cannot tell them how to fix the problem. If the hitter applies the "fixes" found in this chapter they can get out of their slump quickly. If it takes them a long time to make the necessary adjustments, they may find themselves sitting on the bench for awhile. It is important to study the tendencies of the results of the at-bats after each game or two. If the hitter is not having good contact they should make the adjustments found here and the success will follow.

It can be difficult even for the trained eye to see what is wrong with the hitter's fundamentals. Some problems like over striding, stepping out and dropping the hands are obvious. Others are not so obvious. It may appear that the hitter's swing looks great but the results are not. This chapter will delve into the problems when it is not so obvious what the hitter is doing wrong.

Good hitting coaches will analyze the hitter's swing follow through. Noticing the action of the bat head after contact can be an indicator of what the bat did before contact. If the bat seems to be cutting down after contact then the hitter is leaving the barrel behind initially and is making up for it by rolling the wrist at contact. This is a very common problem for the young hitter. Another finish to watch for is the extremely high follow through. If you notice the bat finishing above head high on the follow through then the hitter is probably dropping the back side too much and creating a big upper cutting action. Remember, a shoulder or ear level finish is desired. Finally, if the hitter is constantly letting go with the top hand on the follow through, this may be an indicator of another problem. This concept of letting go with the top hand on the follow through will be discussed in the "Other Hitting Topics" chapter.

Constantly reviewing the fundamentals of hitting and *sticking to the basics* are the best way to avoid developing bad tendencies. This constant review of the mechanics is especially necessary for the hitters who have no one tendency when they hit but never seem to hit the ball solidly. Many of the fundamental mistakes and remedies were covered in the previous chapters. The drills used in those chapters along with some new ones will be used for helping the hitters to get out of their slumps.

There are five results that we will discuss.
1. **Swinging and Missing**
2. **Hitting Nothing but Ground Balls**
3. **Hitting Nothing but Pop Ups and Fly Balls**
4. **Always Pulling the Ball**
5. **Always Late on the Ball**

Problem 1 - Swinging and Missing
Reason # 1 – Bad Timing
Symptom – Always late or always early on the pitch

Obviously, good timing is a must for the hitter. If the hitter's timing is off it usually is noticed by either the hitter herself or the coach. If hitters are consistently late or early, they need better timing.

Bad Timing Remedy 1 – If the hitters' timing is off then there is no substitute for getting out and having a lot of batting practice. Even hitters with great fundamental swings lose their timing from time to time. If the hitter seems to be late more often then not, she needs to face faster, game-like speed. This can be done by hitting fast speeds with a batting machine, having a coach stand closer to home when pitching or facing teammates, all of which approximate game conditions.

If the hitter seems to be early on most swings, then the hitter needs to face slower pitching so that he waits on the ball longer. Remember, there is no such thing as pitching that is too slow or too fast (within reason depending on the age of hitters) during batting practice. It may benefit the hitter if the coach backs up further away from the hitter for batting practice also. This will make the hitter see the ball longer and obviously have to wait longer. Throwing a lot of curve balls and change ups will help the hitter wait longer also.

Bad Timing Remedy 2 – Another reason for poor timing occurs when the hitter does not get the front foot down on time or steps and swings at the same time. Drills # 2, 3, 5, 8, 23, 25 and 27 will help.

Bad Timing Remedy 3 – Many times a hitter's timing gets thrown off because of facing the same speed of pitched ball too often. When they get to a game and the speed is different from what they are constantly practicing, they may struggle. Remember, constantly changing speeds and facing game-like speeds during batting practice is a good thing, even for very young hitters. Hitters need to be careful of hitting the same speed pitch each time they go to the batting cages. Change the speed you are hitting each time you go to the cages.

Bad Timing Remedy 4 – I've noticed that many times a batter's swing is quick enough but his eyes haven't had time to get used to the speed yet. In preseason it is a good idea to start with slower pitching and then gradually increase the speed each time. If the hitter increases speeds too quickly, the hitter may develop bad habits or bad timing because he is not quite ready for the faster speeds yet.

◆ There is a saying among coaches: "It is easier to speed a bat up than to slow it down." This doesn't refer to actual bat speed as the hitter should always be swinging quick and fast. This actually refers to timing. If the hitters' timing is off it is generally easier for them to get used to faster pitching and "speed up their bat" than it is to get their timing back on slower pitching. If hitters are having trouble waiting on the pitch then they are much more vulnerable to slow pitchers and off speed pitches. This is what is meant by being unable to "slow their bat up." This is why it is important to throw slow pitches to the hitters and not all fast ones.

◆ Keeping the front shoulder close to the ball till the very last moment is a must for good contact. This obviously will take good timing and confidence.

Keep those hands up, Jimmy!

Reason # 2 for Swinging and Missing – Swinging under the Ball
Symptom 1 – Dropping the hands

This is a common problem and leads to an upper cutting swing. As the hitter strides she will lower her hands to about waist high. This action will automatically put the bat and hands underneath pitches above the waist. Therefore it is very difficult to hit the higher pitches.

Dropping the Hands Remedy 1 – This is one of the tougher habits to correct and usually will require the use of an obstacle like the batting tee to be placed behind the hitter and a little above the back hip (Drill # 36). With the tee behind the hitter, he will know that his hands have dropped if the bat hits the tee on the forward swing.

Dropping the Hands Remedy 2 – This action of dropping the hands is often associated with the hitter over striding or jumping at the ball. If this is the case the stay back drills in the previous section will help hitters to keep their hands up also. **(Drills # 2, 3, 5, 8, 23, 27, 28, 32, 33.)**

It is much more difficult to ignore the problem of dropping the hands at the lower levels of baseball because the strike zone goes all the way to the letters or a bit higher. In professional baseball the top of the strike zone is called slightly above waist high. Therefore, the professional player learns to lay off this pitch where the young hitter must deal with it. This is all the more reason to keep the hands up when striding.

Symptom 2 – Dropping the barrel in the contact zone

Fastballs are usually missed because the bat is under the ball. If it is a constant problem then the hitter needs to "shorten" the swing. A long swing (see below for a further explanation) means that the bat travels in too long of an arc to the ball. Remember, ideally the bat will gradually level off on the initial portion of the swing. If this is the case the hitter may be dropping the barrel right before contact. When the barrel drops below the ball at the point of contact, the top hand is usually the culprit. Remember, above we mentioned that the front side (lead hand) takes the bat towards the ball and then the back side and top hand will deliver the bat head to the ball at contact. One way of thinking about it is that the lead hand

"That a boy!"

controls the knob of the bat and the top hand will control the bat head. Once again if the bat head is dropping below the ball at contact the hitter needs to do some top hand drills to stay on top and avoid swinging under the ball.

Remedy – The hitter will have to work on keeping the barrel of the bat from dropping under the ball at contact. With young hitters this may be a strength issue and just by choking up on the bat some can solve this problem.

Drills # 29, 44, 45, 46 and 49 are good for this adjustment.

Don't drop that barrel.

Many times you may read in the newspapers that a particular hitter's swing is too long. There are two distances that the bat has to travel to make contact in the ideal zone. This zone is out in front of the hitter towards the pitcher. The bat has to travel the distance between the knees and the distance the hands are back towards the catcher. Every inch the hands or bat barrel move back away from the hitter's back shoulder, the longer the swing. The hands should load to a distance of no more than a couple of inches beyond the back shoulder while maintaining the barrel near the back ear. This should put the hands in the same position that a boxer would make his quickest and most powerful punch from.

The hitter should make contact out front so the bat has to travel the distance between the knees too. The longer the stride or exaggerated wide stance can create a longer swing. The longer the swing the sooner the hitter has to start in order to make contact. This generally means that the hitter is more vulnerable to all pitches because they have to decide to swing on a pitch sooner than the hitter with a compact swing. Many hitters will start the bat in the correct spot but allow the barrel to get away from them as they start the swing. Review the initial paragraphs in "The Fundamentals" chapter which discusses this. The point to be made is that hitters with long swings will struggle as they face better pitching.

The more compact swing will allow the hitter to wait longer on the ball, resulting in better pitch selection and better contact. A few other drills that will help with this "shortening" of the swing are as follows.

Drill # 47 – Pinch the Shirt Drill

The hitters will begin in the set up position by pinching their T-shirt with the thumb and index finger of their top hand with bat in hands. Right before swinging the hitter lets go of the shirt and swings from that point without putting his hands back any further. This will force the hitter to use his hands more and feel the shorter swing as the bat is right next to his back ear. This is a tough drill for real young hitters as they may not have the hand strength to hit from this position. This is an opposite drill leading to a very short swing and greater hand use.

Staying compact and focused.

Drill # 48 – Bounced Ball Drill

The coach from a short distance in front of the hitter and behind a screen will bounce balls up into the strike zone at a pretty good speed. The ball will be rising slightly when getting to the hitting zone and force the hitter to keep the bat barrel from dropping and missing the ball. This will mimic the action of a good fastball that almost appears to rise as it hits the contact area. If the hitters' swing is long, they will be continually under the ball. This drill will help the hitter to shorten the swing and stay on top of the ball more.

Staying on top of the bounced ball.
Get behind the screen, coach.

Double tee will keep the barrel above the ball.

- Physicists say that it is impossible for the ball to rise from an overhand delivery but a good fastball will give this appearance to the hitter's eyes.
- However, in girls' softball there is a definite rise ball. This is a great drill for imitating the action of the rise ball and thus helping the hitter to adjust to this pitch.
- Once again, it is always important for the pitcher to change speeds with the pitches and this can easily be done with this drill by bouncing the ball higher occasionally, which will act like a change up.

Drill # 49 – High, Low Double Tee

Set two tees close together out in front of home plate in the hitting zone. Set a ball on each tee. The ball on the back tee should be a little more than a ball's width below the front tee ball. The object is for the hitters to hit line drives with the front ball while missing the back ball. If the hitter is dropping the barrel at contact it will show up on this drill. Then the hitter can go about doing the drill to fix the problem.

Reason # 3 for Swinging and Missing – Swinging over the Ball
Symptom – Being early on a slow pitch

This is most common on a pitch that is dropping as it gets to the hitting zone, like a curve ball or changeup. The mechanics of the swing may not necessarily be wrong on these pitches. The hitter may have been "fooled" by the pitch and did not wait long enough. If this is happening often the hitter needs to wait longer, and the cure for this is generally shortening the swing as mentioned in the above sections. Simply having more experience at hitting off speed pitches can help, too.

Symptom – Uppercut

Every time hitters uppercut doesn't mean they are under the ball. On a low pitch that the hitter is early on this type of swing will take the bat over the ball. Any swing that does not level off can very easily hit the bottom or top of the ball because it is not on the same plane as the ball.

Remedy – The hitter needs to level out the swing and this is usually done by working on the lead arm drills. The lead hand pull on the first move will put the bat on a much more level plane to the ball. The hitter will need to use more lead arm work in order to prevent the front elbow and shoulder from lifting up.

Drills # 1, 4, 20, 21, 22, 34 and 36 will work to overcome this action.

Collapsing backside — transfer that weight, Jimmy.

On faster pitching the upper cut swing will actually take the bat under the ball because now the hitter will be late on the ball. This is usually caused by the front elbow raising (chicken wing) which will not allow the hitter to take the hands down to the low pitch. The chicken wing concept will be discussed later.

Symptom – Casting

Another reason for swinging over the ball is a common problem that hitting coaches call "casting." This action involves the throwing of the hands and barrel out towards the opposite batter's box on the initial portion of the swing. This action will actually cause the hitter to have to "chop" at the ball. This casting action makes it virtually impossible to hit the back of the ball on any pitch below chest high. The casting will cause the hitter to swing over the top of pitches. Casting is usually caused by a failure to open the hips first before swinging.

Remedy: Drills # 3, 5, 25, 30, and 37 are effective for overcoming this action.

You are probably beginning to realize that two different swings can produce a lot of similar results. That it is why it takes a pretty good trained eye to figure out what the hitter may be doing wrong. The hitter should continually work on a variety of drills so that the muscle memory and hand-eye coordination stay consistent.

Casting out — tough to get to back of the ball.

Problem 2 – Hitting Nothing but Ground Balls

There are two types of ground balls. There is the hard-hit ground ball, which may or may not get through the hole into the outfield, and there are the soft ground balls. With the hard-hit ground ball the hitter is hitting the ball solidly and may only need a slight adjustment in order to turn these into line drives. Weaker and chopped ground balls are obviously more of a problem.

Reason # 1 – Too Many Ground Balls
Symptom – Eye or hand level is too high

The hitter who stands too upright may only be seeing the top half of the ball. The hitter whose hands are too high may be making it more difficult to get the bat to the lower pitches. Keeping the hands at this high level will cause the hitter to either drop the hands or come over the low pitch. Neither of these actions is conducive to a good fundamental swing.

Quick Remedy – If the hitter is making contact but the results are ground balls, the hitter should try these three "quick fixes." Anyone of these may be the answer or it may take all three to fix the problem.

1. The hitter should try widening the stance an inch or two. This will put the hitters' eyes a little lower and will allow them to see and swing to the back of the ball easier.
2. The hitter can try bending the knees a little more for the same reason as stated above.
3. The hitter can lower the hands an inch or two or three. Often the hitter has raised the hands higher than needed, causing her to be unable to get to the back of pitches below the waist. Usually, starting the top hand even or slightly below shoulder level is ideal.

Hands too high — elbows in way.

Reason # 2 – Too Many Ground Balls – Losing Posture During Swing
Symptom – Back leg straightens up

If none of the above three solutions work to solve the problem, the hitter may be rising up with his upper body and head. If the back leg straightens up as the hips rotate, the head and upper body will rise. This causes the level he was intending to swing at also to rise slightly to the point where he now meets the top third of the ball.

Remedy – The hitter needs to keep his head and upper body from rising up as he swings. The hitter should work on a better use of the lower body, especially the bend of the back knee. Filming or putting the hitter in front of a mirror can be very beneficial in order for him to see the back leg action. Remember, the ideal lower half position at contact is the capital A between the legs and not a V. Drill # 42 can really help for the player to see this rising up action during the swing.

Another way of checking for this would be to do Drill # 28. Hitting on the back knee will show the swing without the legs. If the hitter hits line drives on one knee but only ground balls with his regular swing, he is losing *good hitting posture*. Hitting on the back knee will show the hitter that his swing is good and the results of his regular swing would be good if he does not rise up with his swing.

Finish under balance.

- The only time the hitter may have to raise up and straighten the back leg would be to stay on top of the pitch letter high or slightly above. This can help the hitter keep from popping up the high pitch, especially on a hit and run.

- Be sure to review the section above about swinging over the top of balls and missing, also, as this may also help to figure out why the hitter keeps hitting the top of the ball.

- Most of the time when an inexperienced coach sees a lot of ground balls they assume the hitter is chopping down at the ball. Over the years I have run into very few hitters that actually chop at the ball. It is usually the opposite, where the hitter is coming up over the ball and thus hitting choppers because of this.

Reason 3 – Too Many Ground Balls – Bad Contact Position of Hands
Symptom – Palms not parallel to the ground at contact

To square up the ball and bat at contact, the hands should be palm up and palm down at contact. (Review Fundamental # 12 if needed). If the lead hand is facing up or down too much at contact, this can cause the bat to hit the top of the ball also.

Remedy – The following two drills will help.

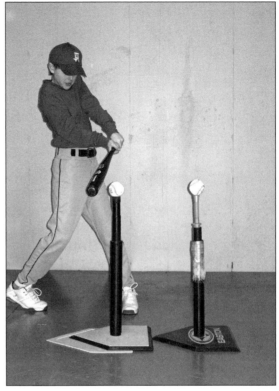

Early roll of wrists prevents power.   *Double tee drill for good posture and extension.*

Drill # 50 – Double Tee Extension

This requires two tees. Set one tee slightly in front of home about thigh high and place the other tee directly in front of this tee at the same height but about a foot in front. Have the hitter swing and try to hit both balls solidly. If the bat starts on an upward arc too soon the result will be a ground ball or chopper on one or both balls. If the hitter maintains good posture and keeps the bat on a level plane, they can hit both balls on the line and solidly. If the wrists roll too early or the swing is an uppercut, the bat will not hit the second ball solidly or at all.

For the power hitter who is continually hitting ground balls – This is not something I recommend for most hitters. As a last resort for a good-sized player with a lot of power the following drill may help.

Drill # 51 – Upper Body Tilt – Mirror

As the hitters are swinging they will tilt back at the waist towards the catcher. This will cause the back shoulder to drop and put an upward arc on the swing. This action is referred to as "back legging it" and has become very popular in this era of the home run hitters. A mirror is a good way to show hitters the tilt of the body that you are trying to show them. This method can produce a lifting of the ball but will make hitters vulnerable to high fast balls and they will have a tendency to hit pop ups.

 This idea will be discussed further in the hitting theories section of this book.

Problem 3 – Hitting Nothing but Pop Ups and Fly Balls

Unless a hitter has tremendous power it usually doesn't pay to hit balls with too much air under them. As a player advances in competition most balls that are hit too high will end up being caught for just another out. If the hitter is making contact but it seems like the ball is always going up, then there are a number of things that may be going wrong. The section above that covers swinging under the ball and missing may provide some answers to this problem, additionally.

Collapsing body will inhibit bat speed.

Reason – Always Hitting the Lower Half of the Ball

Quick Remedy – Along the same lines as the three quick remedies for too many ground balls the hitter can try any or all of the following.

1. Use a narrower stance — this may allow the hitter to see the top of the ball more and avoid the pop up.
2. Take a little bend out of the knees for the same reason as #1 above.
3. Raise the hitter's hand a few inches to see if that helps to stay on top more.

If none of these three quick fixes seem to solve the problem move on to the following remedies.

Symptom – Collapsing the back side

When the ball is hit in the air continually, the bat is obviously only hitting the bottom third of the ball. This is usually caused by some sort of dropping of either the hands or the "collapsing" of the back side. A dropping of the hands was discussed above. Most coaches call the collapsing of the back side "dropping the back shoulder." In reality it is the back knee and hip which break down and causes the back shoulder to dip. The result of this action is a lot of pop ups and fly balls. With the correct swing the back shoulder will drop under the front shoulder some, but the *hips should remain level.* A sign of this collapsing hip is noticing that the hitter is falling in towards home plate upon the completion of the swing.

Remedy – If the problem is on the back side, the solution is usually on the front side. Using more lead arm will help prevent the back side break down.

Along the same lines this breakdown of the back side is also a weight transfer problem. Instead of transferring the weight forward into the direction of the ball, the hitter will allow too much weight to stay on the back leg and this will cause the back shoulder to drop and create more of an uppercut swing. Remember if the hitter's weight is transferred forward more, then the upper body won't tilt back and a more level swing will be the result. To help transfer the weight the lead arm and front side must fire to the ball.

Drills # 3, 4, 10, 22, 51 and 52 will help in transferring the hitter's weight more and thereby avoid the tilting back of the upper body at contact.

Symptom – Bent front leg

At contact the hitter's front leg should straighten and the hitter will hit against a firm front leg. Some hitters allow their front leg to bend at the knee resulting in the lowering of the body and bat at contact. This can cause the hitter to go under the ball, resulting in the pop up. This break down is common on the low pitch. If the hitter uses the back leg correctly the hitter should not have to bend the front knee to get to the low pitch. This break down of the front leg will also diminish bat speed. The following drill and Drill # 22 work best to solve this problem.

Drill # 52 – Standing Tall (No knee bend)

This is another drill that can help the hitter maintain a tall posture and avoid the feeling of collapsing either leg. Have the hitters stand perfectly straight with their feet together. The hitters will swing at balls without bending the knees or striding whatsoever. The hitters also do not use their hips on this drill. This will serve to give the hitters a tall feeling with no break down.

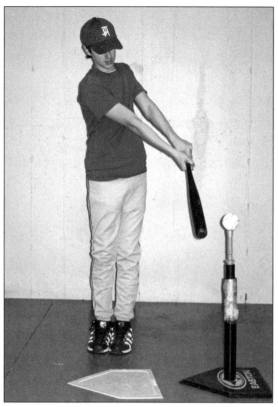

Standing tall — opposite drill.

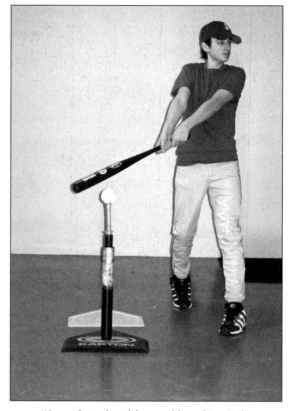

Keep that shoulder and head in, Rob.

Symptom – Pulling out the front shoulder causing an early roll of wrists

Most coaches believe that pop ups are only caused by dropping the hands or back shoulder. This may not be the case. Many balls hit in the air can be caused by the hitter's front shoulder opening either too soon or incorrectly. When the hitter's front shoulder rotates away too early or too much it will cause the wrists to roll early causing the bat to cut underneath the ball. This cutting of the ball will cause the bat to hit the bottom portion of the ball resulting in the ball going up.

Remedy – This generally can be corrected with some front side drills that will keep the front shoulder going towards the ball longer.

Drills # 4, 20, 21, 22, 33 and 52 will serve the purpose.

◆ Drill # 52 explained directly above is also useful for keeping the front shoulder in. Because the hitter doesn't open the hips with this drill the front shoulder will open just slightly. The hitter should concentrate on punching the ball without an early roll of the wrists. This is one of those opposite drills we talked about earlier.

Remember, an opposite drill has the hitters do the opposite of what their normal actions are and then "meet in the middle" when they go back to their regular swings. The hitters will stand totally straight up and swing, hoping to "stay on top of the ball." Obviously, this is not the way we would hit, but it will give the hitters the feeling of keeping their upper body more perpendicular to the ground as they swing. If done enough hopefully the hitters will start to eliminate the dropping of the back side and "meet in the middle."

◆ These front side drills will also serve to get more extension out of the lead arm helping to eliminate an early roll of the wrists.

The Good News

You may be feeling a little overwhelmed by all of these symptoms and solutions. Don't panic, because the good news is that sometimes there are some quick solutions to these problems. If contact is not being made it is obvious more work needs to be done on the fundamentals. With this work and some good batting practice, the contact should follow in time.

If contact is being made but it seems like it is never good contact all is not lost, even if you cannot figure out what the problem may be. What is known is that for whatever reason the hitter is hitting a lot of ground balls. Or, for whatever reason, the hitter is hitting the ball up constantly. Remember, ground balls occur because the bat is hitting the top third of the ball and fly balls occur when the bottom third of the ball is being hit. If the hitter can adjust the swing up or down that one third, then good, solid line drives should be the result. Once again, just by going back to some good fundamental work, the hitter can work his way out of these problems.

Quick remedy for too many ground balls

Because the hitter is not getting to the back of the ball enough, low pitches need to be worked on so that the hands and hips get used to driving to the back of the ball more. The hitter should do a majority of his swings in practice either on the tee, flips or batting practice on low pitches. The hitter should try to continually get behind the low pitch and hit it through the middle or to the opposite field. The best thing to do is to put the tee at the knees and down the middle. Work on hitting line drives back through the middle and over time the hitter will begin to get more solid contact and some lift on the ball. (See Drill #6).

Quick remedy for too many pop ups

The opposite is necessary in order for the hitter to get more on top of the ball. Set the tee up high, even a little above the top of the strike zone. The hitter should work on this pitch until consistent line drives are being hit. This should help the hitter avoid any loop in the swing or an early roll of the wrists. Otherwise, the result will be pop ups. A more compact swing will ultimately be the result of working on these high pitches. (See Drill #7).

◆ Don't totally neglect the other pitch but do a majority of the work on the pitch needed in order to get the necessary results. Maybe fifteen swings at the most needed pitch and then five swings at the opposite pitch would be a good sequence.

◆ You may have noticed that to hit the high pitch consistently the hitter needs to be stronger with the upper body and hands. Along the same line of thinking, to hit the lower pitch the legs and hips are more important. So for too many fly balls, try to have the hitter be more aware of using the *hands,* and for too many ground balls have the hitter think more *hips* with the swing. If you think about it this all makes sense. Using more upper body and hands will allow the hitter to transfer more weight into the ball and stay on top. By using more hips the hitter will have to stay back behind the ball more and have a better chance of lifting it.

Low pitch through the middle. Good job, I knew you could do it.

Way to get on top.

If the hitter can only hit the ball in one direction during batting practice, this is usually a sign of a problem with the swing — the following should help.

Problem 4 – Always Pulling the Ball

The odds of hitting for a consistent high average go down if the hitter is always hitting the ball to the same side of the field as they stand in the batter's box. The best hitters who hit for a high average and with power are hitting the inside back of the ball. That's not to say that there are not some very good hitters that pull the ball often. These type hitters are generally big power hitters who are trying to pull and lift the ball a lot in order to hit home runs. There is really no such thing as the hands being too fast. It is possible that the hitter is early a lot especially on slower pitching but usually there is a mechanical flaw in the swing causing the pulled ball.

Reason # 1 – Going around the ball

Symptom – Chicken wing

When the front elbow rises and the barrel levels off or falls immediately, the elbows will lead the way. When the elbows lead the way instead of the hands, the bat barrel will trail behind. In order to get the bat out front at contact the hitter will roll the wrists early, causing the head of the bat to angle towards the pull side. This was talked about previously and, as mentioned, can cause the pop ups as well.

Remedy – The hitter needs to work on Drills # 1, 4, 21, 34, 36, 44 and 50 in order to get a more compact swing at the beginning. The correct motion of leading with the hands will allow a more extended swing after contact where the wrists will not have to roll early.

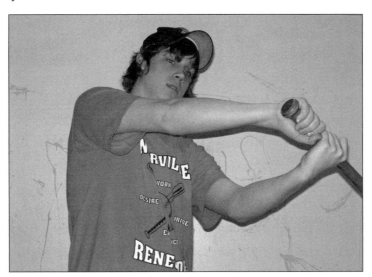

Chicken-winged front elbow will cause barrel to drag behind.

Symptom – Collapsing back side

Another symptom that was mentioned above — the collapsing of the hitter's weight on the back leg — will cause the front shoulder to pull out and thus the pulling of the ball.

Remedy – This is a weight transfer issue. If the hitter can learn to transfer the weight towards the direction of the pitcher and not towards the pull side, the front shoulder will stay in. This will allow the hitter to stay on the outside pitch longer and learn to hit the ball to the opposite field better.

Drills # 3, 4, 10, 21, 22, 43, 50 and 52 will help.

The casting action that was talked about earlier can also cause the hitter to hit the outer half of the ball and thus pull everything. The hitter who casts generally is not opening the hips first but is swinging with the hands before the hips. Drills # 5 and #25 can help the hitter begin the hip rotation before the swing itself.

Problem 5 – Always Late on the Ball

If the hitter can make contact but never can pull the ball then the swing is too long or the front shoulder is opening too soon.

Reason – Hitting the ball too far back in the zone

Symptom – Chicken wing

Here we go again with a particular bad habit causing a different result. When the hitter gets to the level where the pitching gets noticeably faster, the same swing that caused them to always be early can cause them to always be late. The front elbow coming up which is popularly known as a "chicken wing" action will cause the barrel of the bat to drag. This will cause the hitter to be late on the ball. It sounds confusing but the same fundamental problem can cause two different results. Once again the difference between being late or early is the speed of the pitcher or the strength of the hitter. Anytime the elbow leads up, it will put the point of complete extension of the arms out front (towards the pitcher) more and make it tougher to get the barrel out to catch up to good pitching.

Many young hitters are strong enough to get away with the chicken wing and be successful for a number of years, but it will eventually catch up to them.

Remedy – Once again the hitter must work on developing a stronger lead arm to avoid the lifting of the lead elbow on the initial part of the swing.

Drills # 1, 4, 8, 20, 21, 22 and 36 will help this problem to disappear over time.

Symptom for being late – Front shoulder flies open

If the front shoulder opens early, causing the hands to drift forward slightly, the hitter will not be strong enough to get the bat out front. The best way to get the bat out front is to keep the front shoulder closed as long as possible and then fire the lead arm. The back side will come through creating good bat speed and power. The towel drill # 20 is a good start to fixing this. If the front shoulder opens early the hitter will be late often and hitting weak balls to the opposite side. Sometimes this premature opening of the front shoulder will make it tough for the hitter to even swing at some pitches, especially the outside one.

Remedy – The hitter needs to stay relaxed with the front side and keep the hands back longer.

Drills # 2, 8, 33 and 52 will help to keep the shoulder closed and then the hitter will learn how to get the bat out and meet the ball in a timely manner.

◆ Some hitters may be late because they are not getting ready to hit and are very non aggressive. Doing the rhythm Drills # 16, 17, 18 and 19 can help the hitter get ready and definitely be more aggressive.

◆ Notice that one bad fundamental can cause a few different results. The solution, though, is always to get back to the basics and to the drills that reinforce these basics.

▶ *Final Thought* ◀

I know much of this analysis of problem solving can sound confusing because one bad fundamental can cause a few different results. Other factors that determine the results are the speed of the pitches, the hand-eye coordination and physical strength of the hitter. By studying these different reasons, symptoms and solutions, you will greatly enhance your ability to help the hitters. It can give the hitters and coach great satisfaction when they are able to figure out the problem and solve it together.

Too often a "try this, try that" mentality is used where everybody is giving the hitter a solution. The hitters become so confused they don't know what to do. Try to systematically go through the solutions until the proper remedy works. Because hitters have a tendency to fall back into the same bad habit, this remedy will work in the future too. A good review of the "Fundamentals" and the "Advanced Hitting Drills" chapters can obviously help with problem solving also.

10 | **Other Hitting Topics**

"Everything is worth a try — discard what does
not work and try something else"

Good pitching definitely can put a hitter in a slump. The odds favor the pitchers because even the great hitters will make more outs than they get hits. One of my teammates in the big leagues used to say that he felt he needed to hit the ball hard seven out of ten times just to hit .300 in the major leagues. The hitter cannot control whether the hits come or not. The hitter can only control how hard and often he can hit the ball solidly. Sometimes, bad luck comes into play and the balls that are hit solidly get caught for outs. Over time, though, things tend to even out and for every hard hit ball that gets caught there is a weakly-hit ball that finds its way in for a hit.

I knew the pitcher could get me out sometimes, but I believed that I got myself out more often. I was blessed with good hand-and-eye coordination and most of the time I could put the ball in play. This is true for most athletes who have good hand-eye coordination. The difference between success and failure is the hitter's mechanics at home plate combined with the pitches that the hitter chooses to swing at. These are both items that are within the hitter's control. The hitters who develop a good, repeatable swing and learn the strike zone will hit the ball solid those 7 out of 10 times. Hitters who hit the ball hard 7 out of 10 times will be very successful at any level of baseball.

The following are other hitting topics that will tie together many of the ideas put forth in this book.

Hitting Theories

Discussions about different hitting theories usually revolve around a few areas. First is the question of whether the swing is up, down or level. The second area is how the weight shifts — rotational or forward. The third area is whether it is better to let go with the top hand after contact or hang on and finish with two hands on the bat. Let's talk a little about each.

Swing Plane – I believe the swing will involve all three directions, with the down portion beginning the action, followed by the leveling of the bat before the up portion of the swing. This is the correct sequence for a powerful, compact swing. The angle of the body as the bat moves through the hitting zone can cause the bat to change the sequence sooner and will provide more of an upswing. If the upper body tilts back towards the catcher as the hitter swings, the level portion of the swing will be minimized and the up portion will begin much sooner. Instead of the bat being level for an extended period of time, the bat will actually be going up when the bat is out front of the body in the hitting zone. Remember the swing should be just as compact.

Rotational Vs. Forward Weight Shift – Remember in an earlier section we mentioned how the head was the key to our balance. Wherever the head goes our weight will follow. Therefore, where the head is at contact determines where the weight is and this affects the weight shifts of the different hitting styles.

Method 1 – When the hitter rotates the hips and appears to keep much of the weight on the back leg this is a rotational swing. This rotation keeps the head from moving forward at all. This method is often referred to as "back legging it." Although it appears the weight stays on the back leg, in reality the weight does and must shift forward. By keeping the head either back or tilting back as talked about above, the hitter stays totally behind the ball and has the more rotational swing. Hitters who use this method should stand closer to home plate as the front shoulder will open very quickly. They should let the ball get very deep in the zone before swinging. The best example of this swing type is

Tilt back — back legging it.

Ken Griffey Jr. or David Ortiz. This swing will produce a lot of fly balls and a tendency to pull the ball more. Notice this style will generally produce the upswing (as was talked about in the previous paragraph on the swing plane). The down side of this swing style is that it is more difficult to stay on top of the ball and the outside pitch may be a problem if the hitter is not close enough to home plate.

Method 2 – The opposite end of this rotational swing is called front leg hitting. As the pitch is approaching the hitting zone the hitter's weight and head move forward towards the front leg. The back foot actually slides forward slightly with this style. This keeps the front shoulder closed much longer which allows the hitter to stay on top of the ball much easier. It also allows the hitter to handle the

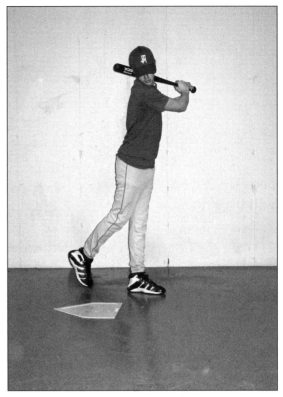

Over front leg head position.

outside pitch, but the inside pitch becomes a little tougher to turn on. This method of hitting produces more ground balls and line drives but less power. Most hitters who use this style have great hands and good speed. The best example of this style is Ichuro Suzuki. This method was more popular thirty years or so ago before the home run craze began.

Recommended head position.

Method 3 – The third method meets in the middle of these two previous styles. The weight shifts with the swing into the ball and the head moves forward a few inches. The angle of the body stays perpendicular to the ground (no tilt). The head remains mostly over the back leg. Remember, with the rotational swing the head and weight stay back more throughout, and with the front leg hitting the weight moves over the front side before the swing. With this third method the hitter keeps the weight back as long as possible but lets it all go with the swing. This method is used by the majority of big league hitters, like Alex Rodriguez (A-Rod) and provides an equal combination of ground balls, line drives and fly balls with power still evident.

Finding the Right Swing for the Hitter

This is where things may be tricky. I talked earlier in this book about a player's natural tendencies. This tilt is one of those. Some hitters will naturally have a little tilt whereas others don't. It can be a problem if the body size doesn't fit this type of swing. Many youngsters have a good swing but it may not be the correct swing for their body and strength levels. As mentioned earlier in the book, it doesn't make sense for a small, fast-running player to use the rotational swing and hit a lot of fly balls and pop ups. Based on the size and skills of the player, the coach should analyze what style of swing may be best for the young player. This may be difficult because it is like a pro scout who must project what a player may be in the future.

Most of the fundamentals discussed in this and most books on hitting teach mainly the third and most conventional method. You cannot go wrong teaching this style. When a player reaches the junior high level the coach should have a good idea of what method of hitting may be best for the hitter, and they may want to try a different style. The change will not be too drastic from the conventional method.

I cannot emphasize enough though that the quick, compact swing is necessary for each method of hitting.

Letting Go with the Top Hand on the Follow Through

There are great hitters who hang on all the way around and great hitters that let go on the follow through. I believe it comes down to personal preference, with a few exceptions. However, it is important for hitters to realize that on every swing they should be able to hang on all the way to the *middle of the back* if asked to do so. Many hitters let go because they are forced to due to an incorrect rotation of the hips or a premature opening of the front shoulder. It is important to find out if the hitters are letting go by choice or if they are forced to let go. The coach can check this by asking the hitters to hold on with two hands for awhile. If they have trouble hanging on with two hands, then they have a fundamental problem that needs to be addressed.

It is important that the letting go of the bat occurs at the right time, also. For the right-handed hitter the letting go should occur around ten o'clock if you picture a clock out front of home plate. For the left-handed hitter this let go will occur around two o'clock. Many hitters let go too soon and thus lose the use of their top hand. The bat barrel will drop resulting in many pop ups.

There may be some advantages of letting go on the follow through for some hitters. One advantage is a lessening of the swing tension. Hitters who let go will tend to throw the bat and thus take some tension out. Hitters who muscle up with the swing may be losing some bat speed. Letting go with the top hand at the right time may actually add a little bat speed for this type of hitter. Another advantage is the hitter can get more extension from the lead arm and thus keep the bat head through that the hitting zone longer without rolling the wrists prematurely. Hitters who are

Top hand let go position.

*Keeping the head in with good extension —
maybe I should have batted right handed.*

much more dominant with their top hand and have a tendency to roll the wrists early can benefit from letting go with the top hand. Often times I would suggest the hitters let go for awhile and compare the results to when they hung on. They can then decide for themselves which way to go. Personally, letting go with the top hand worked great in batting practice but it didn't seem to work for me in the game.

Girls' Fast Pitch Softball Hitting

I have also worked on hitting with a great number of girls. I believe that the fundamentals that a baseball hitter and a softball hitter need are the same. Both hitters need to be able to get the bat out front in the quickest, most efficient and most powerful way possible. In some ways the softball hitter has to be even better fundamentally than the baseball hitter because of three factors. First, the fast pitch softball pitch is very rarely straight. The natural underhand pitch always has top spin on it so the ball will drop as it travels into the strike zone. Also, an accomplished pitcher can make the ball move in all directions, including up. The *rising ball* adds a dimension that the baseball hitter does not have to deal with. Because of this constant movement of the ball it is vital that the softball hitter be able to wait and have as compact a swing as possible. Second, because of the much smaller dimensions of the softball diamond it is more difficult to

You can do it, Jackie.

find holes in the field to get hits. Third, and most obvious, the larger ball used will not go as far or travel as fast off the bat. These factors make it tougher to keep the average as high for many hitters. I believe the drills and methods that have been discussed in this book will help the softball hitter as much as the baseball hitter.

These three factors that make keeping a high batting average in softball more difficult can be overcome somewhat by having superior speed or strength. Girls who have speed can overcome less than ideal fundamentals by using their speed to bunt, slap or beat out ground balls. Girls with a lot of power can enlarge the field somewhat by hitting the ball harder and farther. Having strength is a big advantage because of the ball size but good fundamentals are still necessary to make consistently good contact. Developing hand and forearm strength is necessary for the softball hitter. Fast pitch softball has always been a pitching-dominated game but the hitters are starting to catch up as the hitting coaches are teaching better fundamental hitting to girls at a younger age.

Bunting

In this era it seems like the bunt is becoming more and more obsolete. It can be a great tool for the coach and team, though, as any contact is better than no contact. Also, the sacrifice bunt will always remain a valuable tool at least for the lower levels of ball. The problem with convincing young players to bunt is that in many leagues players may only have one at-bat a game, and to have to bunt their only time up to

See the ball, Jimmy.

bat is not always fair to the player. Many coaches will have their weaker hitters bunt just to make contact and this will not help the youngsters to develop any confidence as hitters. This is not to say that the occasional bunt won't serve to help build confidence. The hitter may get a hit out of the bunt or help the team produce a run and this can help build confidence. This confidence boost can make the player feel like he is contributing to the team's success. The coach should not continually take the bat out of the same player's hands though by always having them bunt.

It is important that the coach gets across the meaning of the "sacrifice" bunt. The hitter is sacrificing himself in order to advance the runner. Make sure he understands that if he put a good bunt down then only good things can occur. If he sacrifices the runner it will not go against the hitter's average. He may even beat it out for a hit which will obviously help the hitter's average.

Sacrifice Bunting Technique

1. **Timing** – When the pitcher's knee is up and ready to move to home plate, the hitter should square around to face the pitcher.

2. **Squaring Around** – This can be done in one of two ways. The hitter can lift his back foot and place it next to the front foot and then slide his front foot over. Or the hitter can simply pivot both feet towards the pitcher. Both methods require the shoulders to turn completely so that they are perpendicular to the pitcher. Either method used to square around should produce the same result of getting the bat out front of the hitter. At this time the hitter's top hand will slide up the bat to the area between the top of the tape and the trademark on the bat. The hitter should close the hand like a fist and then open his thumb up like he is going to press a button with the thumb.

Other points to remind the batter when bunting:

1. The hitter's weight should be on the front leg with the pivot method of bunting and on the foot closest to home with the square around method.

2. The moving-both-feet method is more advantageous for the younger hitters as it will help them get the bat out front easier. As they get older it is more a matter of personal preference as to what method they use.

3. One of the keys to putting a good bunt down is having to not move the bat very far within the strike zone. A good bend of the knees, a slight angle of the bat and compete plate coverage to begin with will ensure this.

4. Hitters should have a good bend in the knees when they square around and place the bat at the top of the strike zone with the barrel end slightly higher than the knob end. The bat should get out in front of the hitter, with the top hand almost straight and the lower hand closer to the body, with the front elbow relaxed close to the body.

5. With the bat starting at the top of the strike zone, the hitter should not have to raise the bat to bunt the ball, except on the suicide squeeze bunt, because the pitch is a ball. Also, the risk of popping the ball into the air is greater on this high pitch.

6. If the hitter knows which line he wants to bunt towards he should angle the bat in that direction when he squares around.

Feet square around bunting method.

Pivot bunting method — notice, bat should get to the same spot with both methods.

7.   **Contact** – The hitter squares the bat to the top, back of the ball with a soft, giving action of the hands.

This should deaden the ball and achieve the objective of advancing the runner.

This may sound easy but it requires a real knack and a lot of practice. When you start to consider the different movements of the pitched ball it becomes even more difficult. The most common mistakes made with bunting are:

1.   **Squaring around too late.** Remember to remind the hitters that this is a sacrifice bunt and you are not trying to fool anyone. It is better to put the bat out too early than to be late and not ready to get a good bunt down.

2.   **Not squaring totally around with the shoulders and thus creating a bad angle of the bat.** A common result of this would be fouling balls off at the hitter's own head or other foul balls.

3.   **Sliding the top hand to an incorrect position.** If the hitter doesn't go up far enough they will not have much bat control and by going up too far on the bat they put their top fingers in danger of being hit by the ball.

4.   **Gripping the bat too tightly or too loosely** makes it hard to "catch" the ball on the bat.

5.   **Standing too tall or with the bat angled up and down too much.** Remember, if the bat has to go a long way to bunt the ball, the chances of squaring up on it are diminished.

6.   **By not putting the bat out front of their body enough,** the hitters will foul off many pitches or jab forward at the ball with the result being either a foul ball or a bunt that is too hard hit.

7.   **Chasing bad pitches.** Remember, the hitter only needs to bunt at strikes unless the suicide squeeze is being deployed.

8.   **Dropping the barrel of the bat right before contact** is a common flaw and can create a popped up bunt.

The suicide squeeze is a sacrifice where the runner from third will break towards home, and it is mandatory that the hitter bunts at the ball and makes contact on any pitch thrown. This is the only situation when the batter will have to bunt at a ball out of the strike zone.

Bunting for the Base Hit

This can be a great source of hits for faster runners. Different from the sacrifice, the hitter is actually bunting to get on base. The key is to wait until the ball is in flight and to only bunt at a good pitch. The bunter still needs to get the bat out front to put the ball down in fair territory. The left handed batter has an advantage here because he is closer to first base to begin with. The batter takes the barrel right by the back ear and out front to the bat angle desired. This bat angle is important to put the ball down the line desired. As the hitter is taking the bat forward, he should shift his weight over his front leg so he is ready to run to first the second the ball is bunted. The hitter needs to work on the timing so he does not give it away too soon or wait too long and foul the ball off. The hitter must be as confident in his bunting as he is with his regular swing in order to be successful. (The coach may have a sign where he suggests the hitter try to get on base with the bunt attempt.)

Even for hitters without good speed, bunting for a base hit can be useful in the following situations.

a) The 1st or 3rd basemen are playing way back and virtually giving the batter the bunt for a hit.

b) The hitter is in a big slump and can really use a hit (any hit).

c) The hitter struggles with off speed pitches. A curve ball and change up are usually easier to bunt because they are slower and already moving downward as they get to the hitter. If the hitter is sure one of these pitches is coming it may be worth a try.

Squeeze Bunt Play

With a runner on 3rd the coach may try to score the runner with a bunt. The hitter's goal is to get the bunt down or at least foul the ball out of play. It is important that the hitter knows for sure that the squeeze bunt sign is on. There should be some signal back to the coach to let him know that the hitter knows to bunt the next pitch. Otherwise this can be a dangerous play if the runner from third is running towards home and the hitter is swinging away. The other thing that is important is that the hitter not square around too soon. If the hitter shows bunt too early this could tip off the pitcher and mess up the play. The hitter should attempt to put the bunt down anywhere in fair territory. As long as the runner left on time any bunt should do the job. Contact must be made on any pitch location or the runner on third will be running into an easy out and thus the name suicide squeeze.

Teaching the runner at third to leave when the pitcher's front foot lands should provide good timing for the play to work.

The Hit and Run

The hit and run is an offensive play where the runner or runners will be running on the pitch. The hitter's goal is to put the ball in play but not in the air where a double play can occur. A ground ball is the desired result so the hitter must be intentional about hitting the top of the ball. The basic swing does not need to change as long as the hitter focuses on staying on top and making contact. The hitter who has the long ball swing should shorten up a little on the swing and concentrate on contact. Any ground ball will usually work. The hitter should just try to go with the pitch and not try to outsmart the defense. The hitter must be aware that contact is a must on this play so he needs to swing at all pitches to protect the runner. The coach should know which hitters to try the hit and run with because some hitters' swings are not conducive to this play. This play is usually used to stay out of the double play or to create a first and third situation. There are times where it may be used to jump start a struggling hitter or team also. The best counts for this are the first pitch, 1 & 0, 1 & 1 and 2 & 1.

Advancing a Runner from 2nd Base to 3rd

The game situation where there is a runner on 2nd base and nobody out usually calls for the hitter to advance the runner to third. The hitter's goal here is to hit the ball to the right side of the field with a ground ball. For hitters with good power a fly ball to right field may also do the job. The hitters must remember that this is not a hit and run so they don't have to swing at everything. The hitters should look for a pitch that they can hit in that direction. Generally, this means a pitch located middle-in for the left handed batter and an outer half pitch for the right handed batter. The advantage of not using the sacrifice bunt in this situation is the opportunity to drive the runner in from second (with a hit to right, for instance).

Sometimes a line drive is the result with the hit and run and the advancing-a-runner situations. This can be good or bad depending on if it gets caught or not. Since line drives are almost always the goal of the hitter, a coach will not get upset if it is caught as he will recognize a great effort but just some bad luck. Sometimes the line drive gets through for a hit with an added bonus of a run batted in or a chance for a big inning.

Hitting a Sacrifice Fly

The game situation where there is a runner on 3rd base with less than two outs calls for the hitter to try and knock this runner home. The goal here is to hit a fly ball deep enough to the outfield to get the runner home. In order to do this the hitter should look for a pitch that they can get into the air. Generally, this means a pitch up in the strike zone, with the key idea being in the strike zone. If the hitter starts chasing pitches that are too high then a pop up to the infield is often the result. The coach should know which of the hitters is capable of hitting deep enough fly balls before recommending that they hit a fly ball. Trying to uppercut the ball in order to lift it usually backfires with the result a strike out or pop up. Just hitting the ball hard is a good philosophy for the hitter without much power in this situation.

Hitting Curve Balls and Change Ups

One of the toughest adjustments that hitters have to make, when they're about 13 years old, is hitting the curve ball and other off speed pitches. I always felt like a good change up was the toughest pitch to hit because there was no change in arc or arm action, making it very hard to pick up. Having a coach or other player throw the hitter a number of curves and change ups can help the hitter's development in this area. In the long run, the key to hitting these pitches is being able to wait on the ball longer. This doesn't mean just waiting on the off speed pitches, but all pitches, including the fast ball. Generally, most hitters will *look for the fast ball and adjust to the off speed pitch*. Hitters who can wait the longest before starting their swing on the fastball will have a better chance of waiting on the other pitches too. The key to waiting longer is having a compact and fundamentally correct swing. Almost every hitter I ever worked with who had major trouble with the curve ball and off speed pitches had a long swing with a fundamental break down. They couldn't wait long enough because their long swing meant they had to start it early on all pitches. This long swing makes them vulnerable to the off speed pitch. The best thing that hitters who have trouble with off speed pitches can do is to work on the fundamental drills which will shorten the swing and allow them to wait longer on the ball.

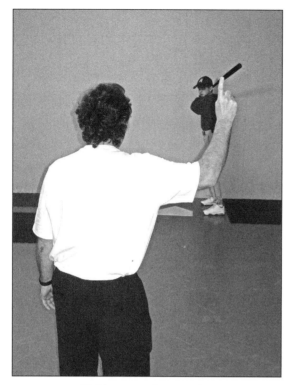
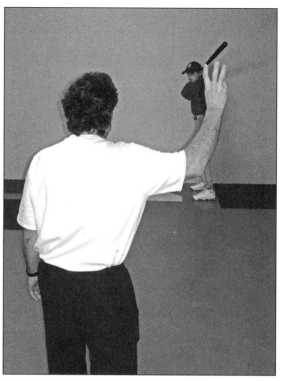

Picking up release point.   *Eyes level and move to release point.*

Vision

Obviously, there is no substitute for having good vision. The player's eyes should be checked before every season to be sure they are up to standards. Doing vision tracking exercises, hitting different colored balls and setting markers along the distance from the pitcher to the hitter can be valuable drills for the hitter. The coach can put different colored spots on the batting practice balls and have the hitters call out the color as soon as they see it. The coach can also set up different markers along the distance between the pitcher and catcher. Have the hitter call out when the ball passes over each marker. This can help to make sure the hitter is watching the ball the complete distance.

Another fun drill to get the hitters focused on the pitcher's release point is to have the pitcher start at a short distance and throw numbers with his fingers (no ball) at the hitter. The pitcher will continue backing up a few steps at a time throwing numbers until the hitters can no longer see them. Making a little contest out of this can be a lot of fun for the team. Obviously, the last player to see the correct number would be the winner. Anything that can get the hitters to focus on the ball more without any distractions can help the hitter to get in the zone.

Pitching Machines

Hitting in batting cages with a pitching machine is good for timing and working on the swing. There is no substitute for real batting practice from a pitcher who changes speeds but this is not always possible. A few tips to make using the batting machine more worthwhile are:

1. Bigger, stronger hitters should not use their expensive aluminum bat because it can wear down quickly, especially if the hard and heavier cage balls are used.

2. The hitters should not start with the fastest pitches. The eyes or hands may not be ready for the speed at first. Hitting fast speeds right away may cause either bad timing or bad fundamentals to develop.

Bunting a round or two can get the hitter used to the speed. Only allow the hitters who know how to bunt correctly to do the bunting, though. It can be dangerous for young hitters who don't know the correct bunting technique.

3. Change the speeds of the machine's pitches as often as possible. It doesn't do any good to hit the same speed for too long only to get to the game where the pitcher is throwing much faster or slower.

4. Change the location of the pitches as often as possible. Some pitching machines are very consistent with their location. If this is the case the hitter should move himself around to have different locations of pitches. For instance, moving closer to the machine or back towards the catcher, the hitter can change the height of the pitched ball. Along the same lines, the hitter should move himself closer and further away from home plate to work on inside and outside pitches.

5. As with regular batting practice, the goal should always be to hit line drives in the direction of the pitched ball.

Switch Hitting

I've had many parents ask me if I thought it was a good idea for their kids to try switch hitting. This is a tough one to answer. I never try to discourage someone from experimenting or trying to improve. However, I do explain to them that hitting is difficult enough from one side and they may be creating two headaches instead of one. It takes a very gifted and dedicated athlete to pull this off, but it can be done. Some factors that may help the decision:

1. I believe it should be a joint decision between the parent and the player to switch hit.

2. There are two possible reasons to want to switch hit. One is that the hitter is a right handed batter and is extremely fast so there is an advantage to hitting from the left side. The other reason is that the curve ball will always be breaking in to the hitters if they switch hit and this can be an advantage. Many times the hitter won't experience curves until about age 13 and then it may be too late to try to switch hit.

3. The determining factor may be the hitter's vision. Many players can swing the bat equally well from each side of the plate but do not necessarily see the ball the same from each side of the plate. If their habits change noticeably when they face a pitcher from the other side of the plate, then the switch hitting idea is not a good one.

4. Players who are intent on switch hitting should work on it for a long period in practice until they are confident that their production won't drop off much before trying it in a game. Most coaches will not want to see the production fall off a great deal compared to what is normal for them.

Lessons, Camps & Clinics

Things are obviously different for young ball players growing up than they were thirty and forty years ago. Kids do not go outside and play baseball like kids did many years ago. If it isn't an organized practice or game, baseball doesn't get practiced and played as much. There are many other sports, video games and activities that consume kids' time. To make up for this it is important for young players who enjoy baseball to participate in instructional programs that help teach the fundamentals and knowledge of the game. The advent of travel leagues in the last few years has also helped with the quality and quantity of baseball being played. Private lessons, group clinics and baseball camps can be a great learning experience for the player. As stated earlier, knowledge can bring confidence for the hitter.

However, sometimes the problem with instruction is that with some hitters knowledge can bring paralysis. The more hitters learn about their swing and hitting, the more they tend to start thinking too much and this can make them *tentative* and appear to be paralyzed. It's important for hitters to realize that they should forget what they have learned when it comes to game time and just watch, time and react to the pitched ball. The good hitting coach should not overwhelm hitters with too many things to think about and should keep reminding them not to think about these things during the game. I just wanted hitters to set up properly in the batter's box and be aggressively relaxed as they watch the ball from the pitcher's hand.

Over time, though, if the hitter has worked on the suggested things the instruction generally will pay off. For the more experienced player, lessons in the off season are the best approach with occasional tune ups during the season. For the younger player, lessons closer to the season, carrying over into the first few weeks of the season, may be best. Sometimes the *benefits of the lessons* showed up more the following year after the hitter took them. I would guess this was because the hitter had more time to acclimate to the changes and stopped thinking about the swing.

Finally, remember the saying, "if it ain't broke, don't fix it." This is important because I never liked working with the students who came in and said that they had 11 hits for their last 14 at bats. I'm thinking, "Why are you here?" When on a roll hitters should just let it ride and not "swing their way out" of a good streak. On the other hand, when hitters are really struggling don't hesitate to get some professional help, for it can save their season and keep them off the bench. Sometimes just a minor adjustment can get the hitter back on track.

Rag Balls

Personally, I liked working with a good, solid but softer ball for batting practice mainly because of safety (mine and the hitter's). Rag balls are great for giving the hitter good curve balls because it is easier to get a rag ball to break. The other advantage is that the coach's arm will not wear out as quickly as when using hard balls. The disadvantage is that it is sometimes difficult for the coach and player to tell if she is hitting the ball solidly or not. I felt like I could challenge the hitters much better with a good softer ball because I could challenge them with faster pitches and by adding curves without the danger of injuring them with bad pitches. The younger the hitter, the more important is the use of a softer ball. The young hitter can obtain a lot of confidence and have a chance to work on her swing without fear. With more experienced hitters a mix of hard balls and rag balls (for curves) is good.

Wood Bats

For the high school player and the serious younger player, it is good to work with a wood bat, especially in the off season. Using a wood bat can build up the hitters' strength and give them a better understanding of when the ball is meeting the sweet spot of the bat. There is less "forgiveness" with a wood bat and obviously they can break. Aluminum bats have a larger sweet spot and almost never break.

The many fall wood bat leagues for high school players have given a greater appreciation of how much more difficult it is to hit with the wood bat. Using it for practice and then being able to go back to the aluminum bat for the games can be advantageous. Fatigue can set in quicker with a wood bat, though, so the hitter must be careful of overdoing it. The closer the season is the more the hitter should get back to swinging the bat that they will use in the games. Despite what some might feel, there is a difference and the hitter shouldn't risk having different timing when going back and forth between wood and aluminum.

To get the real advantage and effect of using the wood bat, a hard ball needs to be used for batting practice.

Bat Speed

If you remember back to the "Problem Solving" chapter of this book you might have noticed that many of the solutions involved front side drills or using the lead arm more. There is a logical reason for this. Most hitters' lead arm is their weaker one. When you think about it most hitters who bat right handed throw right handed. There is a good chance that their left or lead arm is not as strong or agile. I have done some analysis of bat speed using a bat speed meter and some interesting results were found. This analysis was in no way a complete scientific study but rather a study of a few hitters. I do think the trends of this small study may be true for most hitters, though, and may help explain some problem areas for hitters. The findings are:

1. The hitter's stronger arm, which is usually their throwing arm, will swing the bat 8 to 10 miles per hour faster. This probably explains why so many of the problems of hitting are caused by a *weaker lead arm,* assuming the weaker arm is the lead arm like it is for most hitters. This suggests that if hitters can increase the strength and bat speed of their weaker arm they can add bat speed and power.

2. However, when the hitter's strong arm was the top hand the bat speed is the highest. This suggests that right handed players will have the most bat speed if they bat right handed. I was a left handed batter but had more bat speed when swinging right handed. As mentioned in the above section on switch hitting, though, the side that the hitter sees the ball better from is the best side for them to be successful.

3. Bat speed and bat quickness are different. A compact swing will get the bat to the ball quicker than the long swing. Bat speed is not a big factor if it takes the hitter too long to get the bat to the hitting zone. A few years back I did a study of bat speed at a local college. The hitters who had the fastest

bat speed were not the best hitters on the team. They could hit the ball the hardest and farthest if they made contact, but they did not have bat quickness, so their contact was inconsistent.

4.   The hitter's bat speed was the highest on the low pitch. The middle pitch was next and the slowest bat speed came on the letter-high pitch. This suggests that the legs are used more on the low pitch, and the hitter probably gets more leverage on the low pitch because it is further from the hitter's hands. It also suggests that the ball that can be hit the hardest is the lower pitch. This pitch is tougher to get in the air, though.

5.   Every one ounce the bat was lighter corresponded to one mile per hour in bat speed. A much lighter bat can be swung faster. This was the case when the bats were the same length. When the bat size changed the speed difference did not always show up.

6.   There was no noticeable difference when the hitter let go of the bat on the follow through compared to when the hitter hung on. As discussed earlier there might be a difference in bat speed if the hitter has a lot of tension in his swing.

Overload-underload swinging may be very helpful for gaining bat speed. Overload is swinging a heavier bat for gaining strength. Underload is swinging a much lighter bat for speed. The theory is that, over time, the arms will work at the faster speeds when the hitter goes back to his regular bat. The hitter should not put too much added weight on the barrel end of the bat, though, because this could cause the bat to drag through and the slower swing could be counter productive to adding bat speed. The hitter should swing a lighter bat that is close to the same length as his regular bat.

▶ *Final Thought* ◀

I hope you understand now what I meant in the Introduction about how hitting is not as simple as it appears from the sidelines or from watching it on the television. There are many fundamental actions that must be completed in just fractions of seconds. Factor in the movement, speed and control of the pitcher and you see why the advantage goes against the hitter. Then there is the mental side of hitting which is tough to overcome for so many. When the hitter puts all this together there is no better feeling of accomplishment.

11 | Developing the Hitter

"Have fun and have no regrets"

*B*eing a parent of a hitter, or any athlete for that matter, is not always easy. I am a parent and know the ups and downs that come into play during the youngster's playing days. It is important to always keep things in perspective and realize that we cannot relive our careers through our kids. It is difficult to know if we are pushing children to play or they want to play. If baseball is important to you, and that is the sport that you want your child to compete at the most, create a love for the game in your child. Easier said then done, but the following ideas might help.

1. Go to ball games — high school and college games are great because you can bring your gloves along to play a little catch on the side. Usually they are free so if your son or daughter gets antsy you can leave early. Professional games can be expensive but are great because the atmosphere is usually pretty electric and they will make a lasting memory for the young players.

2. Watch baseball on TV. Do not insist that your child watch with you but do call the family in for the "must see" plays.

3. If the child is big into video games, as most are, buy a good video baseball game for her. Play it with them if desired. Any baseball is better than none, especially in the dead of winter.

4. Play ball with your kids often and especially when they initiate the play. Don't constantly instruct, just play. Remember, when you do instruct do so in a matter of fact voice and not in an emotional manner.

5. Try to be as fundamentally correct yourself when you are playing with your kids because they will be following your lead. If your fundamentals are bad they will mimic your actions.

6. Remember the observations made in the "Be the Coach You Were Meant to Be" and the "Having Fun" chapters in this book.

7. Always be positive and optimistic. Remember to recognize the effort level and not the results. The results can improve over time with practice and patience. If the effort level is not there then the love may not be there and that is not something you can control. Don't forget that "false praise" is not necessary, though. "Get em next time" is better than "you were awesome" after a tough game.

8. Pray for caring coaches.

9. Outside of the team, instructional programs (camps, clinics and lessons) are great. Check to make sure it is a quality program and your son or daughter wants to go. Don't force them to go but encourage them to consider it.

Practice tips for developing the hitter by age

Ages 4 to 6
1. The big-barrel whiffle bat is great to begin the player's career. Use more than one ball if you don't have a catcher.

2. Pitch underhand at a close range — *avoid the arc* on the ball if possible even at this age. There is no reason to teach anything except for how to hold the bat, feet alignment and "watch the ball." You don't have to insist on these either at this age if they don't pick it up right away — allow a little leeway and keep things moving.

3. Show excitement when they do hit the ball and set up a base to run to. Kids this age love to run and it doesn't matter what direction at this age. You may have to try to hit their bat if they are not hitting it. Notice where their swing path is and aim there.

4. Only play as long as your child is interested.

5. Tee ball leagues are fine but pitch to your player if possible in practice.

Ages 7 to 9

1. Stay with a softer ball if possible. Use a tee ball bat or appropriate size bat for age (see "The Fundamentals" chapter for a bat size chart).

2. Overhand pitching is fine but once again avoid the arc on the ball. Pitching on a knee is good because it will help avoid the arc and be more like the pitches coming from kids of that age.

   An arc on the pitch will promote an uppercut swing and this will not be good when the hitter moves up in age and level.

3. Provide instruction — keep it simple, though, and allow for mistakes and failure.

4. When contact becomes consistent begin to challenge the hitter with faster speeds so the hitter doesn't get comfortable with developing a long swing.

5. Begin the session with some regular swings followed by some drills found in the "Five Drills to Teach the Fundamentals" section. Stay attentive to detail, making sure the drill is done as fundamentally, correct as possible. Over time, as the drills become easier for the hitters you will notice their regular swing is looking smoother. Review and observe the tips given in the "Instant Feedback" chapter of this book.

6. This is a good age to encourage some outside instruction if the young player is interested and you feel like it will help your son or daughter. Attend the sessions with them if possible. You will remember more than the youngster and will *recognize if your kids are enjoying it* or not. If they are not having fun at the session wait for a later age to begin with outside instruction.

7. Coach pitch and machine pitch leagues are good for this age especially for the more tentative player.

8. Use of a tee as a hitting improvement device can be used at this age and should be used for the rest of their career for swing improvement.

Ages 10 to 12

1. Use of a softer ball or a mix of hard balls and softballs are good at this age.

2. This is the age to really challenge the hitter. It is not uncommon for hitters at this age to see upwards of 50 miles per hour and some off speed pitches.

3. A few professional lessons before the season may be a good idea if the player is interested. Getting off to a good start can make or break the player's season and confidence level.

4. After the hitter gets proficient at the basic drills provided (# 1–8) begin with some advanced drills (# 9–52).
5. Try to find the drill or two that addresses the hitter's particular problem area.
6. Some off season programs for the serious player are a good idea at this age.
7. Full time travel baseball or a limited travel program can be considered at this age.

Ages 13 to 14

1. If making the high school team is the objective, then it is time to work on their game for 9 months of the year.
2. Conditioning programs and speed training should be considered at this age. Size, speed and strength are big factors in making the high school team. Players cannot do anything about size but can do a lot for speed and strength.
3. The better players should attend the local high school's camps or clinics. Weaker players may want to stay away and work harder on their skills. Players get labeled early and it may work against them if their skills or size is not up to standards yet. Keep working and take your chances at the tryout.
4. Professional lessons and a tee set up at home are recommended.
5. Travel baseball is an option but not mandatory.
6. All drills in this book and an understanding of the ideas put forth in the "Coach Talk," "Mental Side of Hitting" and "Other Hitting Topics" chapters should be practiced and studied by the hitter.
7. Encourage the players to work as hard as possible so whatever the future results, the players will have no regrets about not giving it their best.

High School and Above

1. A good understanding and continual practice of the ideas and drills put forth in books like this are good.
2. Strength and conditioning programs are a must.
3. Even if the players don't make the high school team, encourage them to keep playing in the local summer leagues.
4. Nine months of practice on the skills with a 3-month break should be done at this level. Hitters should have a workable tee set up at home to make daily adjustments if needed.

5. Off season private lessons and lessons at struggling times during the season are recommended. Taking a lesson from a different coach from time to time may be helpful also. Sometimes, when a player hears the same instruction terms, time after time, the words go in one ear and out the other. Another hitting coach may pick up on something else also. Stay away from drastic changes, though, during the season. The off season is a better time to make a big change in the swing mechanics.

6. Consider college camps and showcases at this age at least to get an idea of where the player stands.

7. Fall wood bat league should be considered and is recommended.

▶ *Final Thought* ◀

Playing in the major leagues was a dream come true for me. When I look back, though, the fun part was the journey getting to that level. The work put into it, the day-to-day challenges, the friendships made and the striving for the goal were the most exciting things. Every young player a coach comes across has dreams, whatever they may be. The coach and the game of baseball can provide the means to understand how to reach those dreams. By teaching players the work ethic necessary to be successful and helping them meet the little challenges the game presents helps to mold their future. Furthermore, being a friend and a role model will help them throughout their journeys. Best of luck.

Drill #	Name	Page #	Reason For Drill
1	Pad Drill	40	Establish Hitting Position, Force Hands to be used; Avoid Chicken Wing
2	Fake Flip Drill	41	Maintaining or going to Hitting Position at front foot Landing
3	Fast Knee Drill	42	Staying Back, Correct First Move, Opening Hips Fast
4	Pull, Pivot, Push Drill	43	Using Front Side, Throwing Hands, Keeping Front Shoulder In; Extension, Weight Transfer
5	1,2,3,4 Drill	45	Making Sure Each Phase of Swing sequence is Correct
6	Knee High Pitch	56	For Correct Mechanics, Squaring up Hands Through Middle and Hips
7	High Tee	56	Compact Swing, Eliminating Uppercut Swing
8	Dropped Balls	58	Staying Back, Compact Swing, Swing Plane
9	Balance Beam	74	Stance and Feet Alignment, Correct Setup
10	Swing Balance	77	Balance, Balance, Balance
11	Hold Bat with One Arm – Alternating Hands	78	Establishing Correct Hitting Position
12	Weighted Bat	78	Maintaining Good Hitting Position
13	Front Shoulder Load	81	Preparing to Swing
14	Hitch or Hand Load	81	Preparing to Swing
15	Knee Tuck	82	Getting Weight Back, Preparing to Swing
16	Rhythm-Trigger Drill 1	82	Preparing to Hit, Rhythm and Weight Shift Back

Drill #	Name	Page #	Reason For Drill
17	Rhythm-Trigger Drill 2	83	Preparing to Hit, Rhythm and Weight Shift Back
18	Rhythm-Trigger Drill 3	83	Preparing to Hit, Rhythm and Weight Shift Back
19	Rhythm-Trigger Drill 4	84	Preparing to Hit, Weight Shift, Developing Aggressiveness
20	Snap Towel Drill	85	Avoiding the Step Out, Using Front Side, Quick Hands
21	Lead Arm Swings	86	Avoiding the Step Out, Strong Front Side, Lead Arm Action
22	Back Knee Pick Up	86	Front Side Drill, Good 1st Move, Avoiding Weight Transfer; Collapse of Back Side
23	No Stride	87	Avoiding Problems with Stride, Staying Back
24	Stride Direction Barrier	88	Stride Direction, Keeping Stride Under Control
25	Inside, Outside Tee	88	Consistent Stride, Understanding Points of Contact
26	Standing on Bench Drill	90	Controlled Stride, Balanced Swing
27	Obstacle In Front of Lead Foot	90	Controlled Stride, Avoiding the Lunge
28	On the Back Knee	92	Staying Back, Using Hands, Steady Head, Isolate Upper Half
29	Top Hand Hitting	92	Barrel Control, Staying Behind Ball, Using Back Side
30	Hip Turns	93	Hip Rotation, Developing Faster Hips, Weight Transfer
31	Head Back	93	Avoid Lunging & Over striding, staying behind Ball

Drill #	Name	Page #	Reason For Drill
32	Net Close behind Hitter	94	Staying Back, Using Hips, Avoid Lunging
33	Behind the Hitter Soft Toss	95	Staying Back, Extension, Keeping Head In & Down
34	Net Close behind Hitter Version 2	96	Correct 1st Move, Compact Swing, Using Hands & Hips
35	Net Drill to Avoid Reaching	97	Staying Inside the Ball, Avoid Casting, Using Hips to Open
36	Tee behind Hitter	97	1st Move, Compact Swing, Avoid Long Swing & Uppercut
37	Pad under Back Elbow	98	Avoid Casting, Staying together on 1st move
38	Modified Batting Practice	99	Bat Control, Correct Contact Position
39	Outside Pitch Tee Work	99	Correct Swing on Outside Pitch, Palm Up Palm Down Contact
40	Freeze Balance Drill	100	Overall Balance, Correct Finish
41	Head Down at Contact	100	Head & Eyes On Ball at Contact, Tracking Ball
42	Head Position – Video	101	Controlling the Head, Keeping on Plane
43	Rapid Fire	102	Balance, Correct & Fast Hips, Quick Hands, Compact Swing
44	Dropped Ball	102	Compact Swing, Staying Relaxed but Ready
45	Self Flips	103	Developing Quick & Strong Hands, Bat Control, Short Swing
46	Two Ball Flips	104	Waiting for Ball, Staying Back with Confidence, Compact Swing

Drill #	Name	Page #	Reason For Drill
47	Pinch the Shirt Drill	134	Avoiding Locked Out Front Arm, Developing Forearm Strength
48	Bounced Ball Drill	135	Staying Compact & on Top, Avoiding the Uppercut
49	High, Low Double Tee	136	1st Move, Barrel Control, Avoid Uppercut
50	Double Tee Extension	141	Level Swing, Good Extension, Staying through Hit Zone
51	Upper Body Tilt – Mirror	142	Staying Behind Ball, Creating Lift
52	Standing Tall (No knee bend)	143	Staying On Top, Using Hands, Avoid – Collapse, Extension

About The Author

Playing major league baseball from 1980 to 1986 was a dream come true for Jack Perconte. An even greater thrill was teaching young players for the past twenty years the baseball and softball skills necessary to reach their potential.